To

_____

From

_____

Date

_____

Just for Kids

365 Daily Devotions

Scripture quotations are taken from:

The Holy Bible, King James Version

The Holy Bible, New International Version (NIV) Copyright © 1973, 1978, 1984, by International Bible Society. Used by permission of Zondervan Publishing House. All rights reserved.

The Holy Bible, New King James Version (NKJV) Copyright © 1982 by Thomas Nelson, Inc. Used by permission.

The New American Standard Bible®, (NASB) Copyright © 1960, 1962, 1963, 1968, 1971, 1972, 1973, 1975, 1977, 1995 by The Lockman Foundation. Used by permission.

Holy Bible, New Living Translation, (NLT)copyright © 1996. Used by permission of Tyndale House Publishers, Inc., Wheaton, Illinois 60189. All rights reserved.

The Message (MSG)- This edition issued by contractual arrangement with NavPress, a division of The Navigators, U.S.A. Originally published by NavPress in English as THE MESSAGE: The Bible in Contemporary Language copyright 2002-2003 by Eugene Peterson. All rights reserved.

New Century Version®. (NCV) Copyright © 1987, 1988, 1991 by Word Publishing, a division of Thomas Nelson, Inc. All rights reserved. Used by permission.

The Holman Christian Standard Bible™ (HCSB) Copyright © 1999, 2000, 2001 by Holman Bible Publishers. Used by permission.

International Children's Bible®, New Century Version®. (ICB) Copyright © 1986, 1988, 1999 by Tommy Nelson™, a division of Thomas Nelson, Inc. All rights reserved. Used by permission.

Cover Design and Page Layout by Bart Dawson

ISBN 1-58334-362-8

Printed in the United States of America

Just for Kids

365 Daily Devotions

A Message for Parents

Perhaps your child's bookshelf is already filled with an interesting, spirit-lifting collection of children's books. If so, that means you're a thoughtful parent who understands the importance of reading to your young child. And if you treasure the time you spend reading to your youngster, this text can be an extremely important addition to your child's library.

This book (which is intended to be read by Christian parents to their young children) contains 365 brief chapters, one for each day of the year. Many chapters have been taken from the popular "Little Book Devotions" series, a collection of kid-friendly essays on topics such as kindness, honesty, forgiveness, and self-control. Other chapters contain notable Bible verses which can be discussed—and perhaps memorized—by your child. Still other chapters contain "Big Ideas" which are easy-to-understand quotations from notable Christian thinkers.

If, during the coming year, you read this book to your child, you'll enjoy 365 different opportunities to share God's wisdom with your son or daughter, and that's a very good thing.

If you have been touched by God's love and His grace, then you know the joy that He has brought into your own life. Now it's your turn to share His message with the boy or girl whom He has entrusted to your care. Happy reading! And may God richly bless you and your family now and forever.

The Bread of Life

Then Jesus said, "I am the bread that gives life.
Whoever comes to me will never be hungry,
and whoever believes in me
will never be thirsty."

John 6:35 NCV

Who's the best friend this world has ever
had? Jesus, of course! When you invite Him
into your heart, Jesus will be your friend, too
. . . your friend forever.

Jesus has offered to share the gifts of
everlasting life and everlasting love with the
world . . . and with you. If you make mistakes,
He'll still be your friend. If you behave badly,
He'll still love you. If you feel sorry or sad, He
can help you feel better.

Jesus wants you to have a happy, healthy
life. He wants you to be generous and kind. He
wants you to follow His example. And the rest
is up to you. You can do it! And with a friend
like Jesus, you will.

How to Start Your Day

It is good to give thanks to the Lord,
to sing praises to the Most High. It is good to
proclaim your unfailing love in the morning,
your faithfulness in the evening.

Psalm 92:1-2 NLT

How do you start your day? Do you sleep till
the last possible moment without giving a single
thought to God? Hopefully, that's not the case.
If you're smart, you'll start your day with a
prayer of thanks to your Heavenly Father.

Each new day is a gift from God, and if
you're wise, you'll spend a few quiet moments
thanking the Giver. It's a wonderful way to
start your day.

A Thought for Today

Surrender your mind to the Lord at the
beginning of each day.

Warren Wiersbe

Wise Choices

I am offering you life or death, blessings or
curses. Now, choose life! . . .
To choose life is to love the Lord your God,
obey him, and stay close to him.

Deuteronomy 30:19-20 NCV

Choices, choices, choices! You've got so
many choices to make, and sometimes, making
those choices isn't easy. At times you're torn
between what you want to do and what you
ought to do. When that happens, it's up to you
to choose wisely . . . or else!

When you make wise choices, you are
rewarded; when you make unwise choices, you
must accept the consequences. It's as simple
as that. So make sure that your choices are
pleasing to God . . . or else!

Today's Tip

Wise choices bring you happiness; unwise
choices don't. So whenever you have a choice
to make, choose wisely.

Your Attitude

Make your own attitude that of Christ Jesus.
Philippians 2:5 HCSB

What's an attitude? The word "attitude" means "the way that you think." And don't forget this: your attitude is important.

Your attitude can make you happy or sad, grumpy or glad, joyful or mad. And, your attitude doesn't just control the way that you think; it also controls how you behave. If you have a good attitude, you'll behave well. And if you have a bad attitude, you're more likely to misbehave.

Have you spent any time thinking about the way that you think? Do you pay much attention to your attitude? Hopefully so! After all, a good attitude is better than a bad one.

You have more control over your attitude than you think. So do your best to make your attitude a good attitude. One way you can do that is by learning about Jesus and about His attitude toward life. When you do, you'll learn that it's always better to think good thoughts, and it's always better to do good things.

Celebrate!

Celebrate God all day, every day.

Philippians 4:4 MSG

Do you feel like celebrating? Hopefully so!
Are you expecting God to do wonderful things?
Hopefully so! Are you happy about your family,
your friends, and your church? Hopefully so!
After all, God loves you, and that fact should
make you very happy indeed. So treat this day
as a big celebration . . . because that's exactly
what it should be.

A Thought for Today

All our life is a celebration for us; we are
convinced, in fact, that God is always
everywhere. We sing while we work . . . we pray
while we carry out all life's other occupations.

St. Clement of Alexandria

Today, Try to Memorize This Verse

For God so loved the world that
He gave His only begotten Son,
that whoever believes in Him
should not perish
but have everlasting life.

John 3:16 NKJV

Here's a Bible verse that you should learn.
Practice saying it several times.
And then, talk to mom or dad
about exactly what the verse means.

God Wants You to Share

Be devoted to one another in brotherly love.
Honor one another above yourselves.
Romans 12:10 NIV

You've heard it plenty of times from your parents and teachers: share your things. But it's important to realize that sharing isn't just something that grown-ups want you to do. It's also something that God wants you to do, too.

The word "possessions" is another way of describing the stuff that belongs to you: your clothes, your toys, your books, and things like that are "your possessions."

Jesus says that you should learn how to share your possessions without feeling bad about it. Sometimes, of course, it's very hard to share and very easy to be stingy. But God wants you to share—and to keep sharing! Since that's what God wants, it's what you should want, too.

Making Things Better

For out of the overflow of the heart
the mouth speaks.

Matthew 12:34 NIV

When we're frustrated or tired, it's easier to speak first and think second. But that's not the best way to talk to other people. The Bible tells us that "a good person's words will help many others." But if our words are to be helpful, we must put some thought into them.

The next time you're tempted to say something unkind, remember that your words can and should be helpful to others, not hurtful. God wants to use you to make this world a better place, and He will use the things that you say to help accomplish that goal . . . if you let Him.

A Thought for Today

Happy the man whose words issue from the
Holy Spirit and not from himself.

Anthony of Padua

The Courage to Tell the Truth

And you shall know the truth,
and the truth shall make you free.
John 8:32 NKJV

Sometimes, we're afraid of what might happen if we tell the truth. And sometimes, instead of doing the courageous thing, we do the unwise thing: we lie.

When we're fearful, we can and should find strength from friends, from family members and from God.

So, if you're afraid to tell the truth, don't be! Keep looking until you find the courage to be honest. Then, you'll discover it's not the truth that you should be afraid of; it's those troublesome, pesky lies!

A Thought for Today

Only Jesus Christ is the truth for everyone who has ever been born into the human race, regardless of culture, age, nationality, generation, heritage, gender, color, or language.

Anne Graham Lotz

It's Easy to Worry

The Lord himself will go before you.
He will be with you; he will not leave you or
forget you. Don't be afraid and don't worry.
Deuteronomy 31:8 NCV

It's easy to worry about things—big things and little things. But the Bible promises us that if we learn to trust God more and more each day, we won't worry so much.

Are you worried about something? If so, try doing these two things: first, ask God for His help. And second, talk things over with your parents. When you do these things, you won't worry so much. And that's good . . . VERY good!

Today's Tip

Worried about something you said or did? If you made a mistake yesterday, the day to fix it is today. Then, you won't have to worry about it tomorrow.

Today, Try to Memorize This Verse

And remember,
I am with you always,
to the end of the age.

Matthew 28:20 HCSB

Here's a Bible verse that you should learn.
Practice saying it several times.
And then, talk to mom or dad
about exactly what the verse means.

Forgive Quickly

Be even-tempered, content with second place,
quick to forgive an offense. Forgive as quickly
and completely as the Master forgave you.
And regardless of what else you put on,
wear love. It's your basic, all-purpose garment.
Never be without it.

Colossians 3:13-14 MSG

When you make a mistake or hurt someone's
feelings, what should you do? You should say
you're sorry and ask for forgiveness. And you
should do so sooner, not later.

The longer you wait to apologize, the harder
it is on you. So, if you've done something wrong,
don't be afraid to ask for forgiveness, and
don't be afraid to ask for it NOW!

Today's Tip

Forgiving other people is one way of
strengthening your relationship with God.

Friendships Can Be Wonderful

If you've gotten anything at all out of following
Christ, if his love has made any difference in
your life, if being in a community of the Spirit
means anything to you, if you have a heart,
if you care—then do me a favor:
Agree with each other, love each other,
be deep-spirited friends.

Philippians 2:1-2 MSG

The Bible tells us that friendship can be a
wonderful thing. That's why it's good to know
how to make and to keep good friends.

If you want to make lots of friends,
practice the Golden Rule with everybody
you know. Be kind. Share. Say nice things. Be
helpful. When you do, you'll discover that the
Golden Rule isn't just a nice way to behave; it's
also a great way to make and to keep friends!

Today's Tip

If you want to make more friends, how can you
do it? Try this: First, become more interested
in them... and pretty soon they'll become more
interested in you!

Share Your Blessings

Remember this: the person who sows sparingly
will also reap sparingly, and the person who
sows generously will also reap generously.
2 Corinthians 9:6 HCSB

Jesus told us that we should be generous
with other people, but sometimes we don't feel
much like sharing. Instead of sharing the things
that we have, we want to keep them all to
ourselves. But God doesn't want selfishness to
rule our hearts; He wants us to be generous.

Are you lucky enough to have nice things?
If so, God's instructions are clear: you must
share your blessings with others. And that's
exactly the way it should be. After all, think
about how generous God has been with you.

Today's Tip

There is a direct relationship between
generosity and joy—the more you give to
others, the more joy you will experience for
yourself.

Love That Never Fails

The unfailing love of the Lord never ends!
Lamentations 3:22 NLT

How much does God love you? He loves you so much that He sent His Son Jesus to come to this earth for you! And, when you accept Jesus into your heart, God gives you a gift that is more precious than gold: that gift is called "eternal life" which means that you will live forever with God in heaven!

God's love is bigger and more powerful than anybody can imagine, but it is very real. So, do yourself a favor right now: accept God's love with open arms and welcome His Son Jesus into your heart. When you do, your life will be changed today, tomorrow, and forever.

A Thought for Today

As God's children, we are the recipients of lavish love—a love that motivates us to keep trusting even when we have no idea what God is doing.
Beth Moore

Big Ideas About...

Wisdom

Here are two important ideas.
Take a few minutes to talk to your mom or dad
about what these quotations mean.

If you lack knowledge,
go to school.
If you lack wisdom,
get on your knees.

Vance Havner

Wisdom is the right use of knowledge.
To know is not to be wise. Many men know
a great deal, and are all the greater fools for it.
But to know how to use knowledge
is to have wisdom.

C. H. Spurgeon

How Would Jesus Behave?

Follow Me, He told them, "and I will make you fishers of men!" Immediately they left their nets and followed Him.

Matthew 4:19-20 HCSB

If Jesus were here, how would He behave? He would be loving and forgiving. He would worship God with sincere devotion. He would serve other people, and He would always abide by the Golden Rule. If Jesus were here, He would stand up for truth and speak out against evil.

We read in the Bible that Jesus wants each of us to do our best to be like Him. We can't be perfect Christians, but we can do our best to obey God's commandments and to follow Christ's example. When we do so, we bring honor to the One who gave His life for each of us.

A Hopeful, Hope-filled Heart

I wait for the Lord;
I wait, and put my hope in His word.
Psalm 130:5 HCSB

Are you a hope-filled kid? Hopefully so! When you stop to think about it, you have lots of reasons to be hopeful: God loves you, your family loves you, and you've got a very bright future ahead of you. So trust God, and be hopeful. When you do, you'll be a happier person . . . and God will smile.

Today's Tip

Don't give up hope: Other people have experienced the same kind of hard times you may be experiencing now. They made it, and so can you.

Your Most Important Book

For I am not ashamed of the gospel,
because it is God's power for salvation to
everyone who believes.

Romans 1:16 HCSB

What book contains everything that God
has to say about His rules and His Son? The
Bible, of course. If you read the Bible every
day, you'll soon learn how God wants you to
behave.

Since doing the right thing (and the smart
thing) is important to God, it should be
important to you, too. And you'll learn what's
right by reading the Bible.

The Bible is the most important book you'll
ever own. It's God's Holy Word. Read it every
day, and follow its instructions. When you do,
you'll be safe now and forever.

Today's Tip

Read the Bible? Every day! Try to read your
Bible with your parents every day. If they
forget, remind them!

A Cheerful Heart

For the happy heart, life is a continual feast.
Proverbs 15:15 NLT

What is a continual feast? It's a little bit like a non-stop birthday party: fun, fun, and more fun! The Bible tells us that a cheerful heart can make life like a continual feast, and that's something worth working for.

Where does cheerfulness begin? It begins inside each of us; it begins in the heart. So today and every day, let's be thankful to God for His blessings, and let's show our thanks by sharing good cheer wherever we go. This old world needs all the cheering up it can get . . . and so do we!

A Thought for Today

When we bring sunshine into the lives of others, we're warmed by it ourselves. When we spill a little happiness, it splashes on us.
Barbara Johnson

Slowing Down for God!

Don't burn out; keep yourselves fueled
and aflame. Be alert servants of
the Master, cheerfully expectant.
Don't quit in hard times; pray all the harder.

Romans 12:11-12 MSG

Everybody knows you're a very busy kid. But
here's a question: are you able to squeeze time
into your schedule for God? Hopefully so!

Nothing is more important than the time
you spend with your Heavenly Father. So, take
some time today and every day to pray and to
thank God for His blessings. God will be glad
you did, and you'll be glad, too.

A Thought for Today

Half an hour of listening to God is
essential except when one is very busy.
Then, a full hour is needed.

St. Francis of Sales

God's House

For where two or three are gathered together in My name, I am there among them.

Matthew 18:20 HCSB

When your parents take you to church, are you pleased to go? Hopefully so. After all, church is a wonderful place to learn about God's rules.

The church belongs to God just as surely as you belong to God. That's why the church is a good place to learn about God and about His Son Jesus.

So when your mom and dad take you to church, remember this: church is a fine place to be . . . and you're lucky to be there.

Today's Tip

Forget the excuses! If somebody starts making up reasons not to go to church, don't pay any attention . . . even if that person is you!

You're One-of-a-Kind

You're blessed when you're content with just
who you are—no more, no less. That's the
moment you find yourselves proud owners of
everything that can't be bought.

Matthew 5:5 MSG

When God made you, He gave you special
talents and opportunities that are yours and
yours alone. That means you're a very special,
one-of-a-kind person, but that doesn't mean
that you should expect to be perfect. After
all, only one earthly being ever lived life to
perfection, and He was, of course, Jesus.
Jesus loves you even when you're not perfect.
Your parents feel the same way. And if all
those people love you, you should love yourself,
too.

A Thought for Today

Because we are rooted and grounded in
love, we can be relaxed and at ease, knowing
that our acceptance is not based on our
performance or our perfect behavior.

Joyce Meyer

Keep The Peace

Love must be without hypocrisy. Detest evil;
cling to what is good. Show family affection to
one another with brotherly love.
Outdo one another in showing honor.
Romans 12:9-10 HCSB

Sometimes, it's easiest to become angry with
the people we love the most. After all, we know
that they'll still love us no matter how angry we
become. But while it's easy to become angry at
home, it's usually wrong.

The next time you're tempted to become
angry with a brother, or a sister, or a parent,
remember that these are the people who love
you more than anybody else! Then, calm down.
Because peace is always beautiful, especially
when it's peace at your house.

Today's Tip

What if you're having really big problems with
your family? If so, you've simply got to keep
talking things over, even if it's hard. And,
remember: what seems like a mountain today
may turn out to be a molehill tomorrow.

Let's Be Patient

Knowledge begins with respect for the Lord,
but fools hate wisdom and self-control.
Proverbs 1:7 NCV

The Bible tells us that we should be
patient with everybody, not just with parents,
teachers, and friends. In the eyes of God, all
people are very important, so we should treat
them that way.

Of course, it's easy to be nice to the people
we want to impress, but what about everybody
else? Jesus gave us clear instructions: He said
that when we do a good deed for someone less
fortunate than we are, we have also done a
good deed for our Savior. And as Christians,
that's exactly what we are supposed to do!

Today's Tip

Speak respectfully to everybody, starting with
parents, grandparents, teachers, and adults
. . . but don't stop there. Be respectful of
everybody, including yourself!

Learning to Control Yourself

But endurance must do its complete work,
so that you may be mature
and complete, lacking nothing.
James 1:4 HCSB

If you're having trouble learning how to control your actions or your emotions, you're not alone! Most people have problems with self-control from time to time, so don't be discouraged. Just remember that self-control requires practice and lots of it. So if you're a little discouraged, don't give up. Just keep working on improving your self-control until you get better at it. . . . and if you keep trying, you can be sure that sooner or later, you will get better at it.

A Thought for Today

If things are tough, remember that every flower that ever bloomed had to go through a whole lot of dirt to get there.
Barbara Johnson

Big Ideas About . . .

Jesus

Here are two important ideas.
Take a few minutes to talk to your mom or dad
about what these quotations mean.

When we are in a situation
where Jesus is all we have,
we soon discover he
is all we really need.

Gigi Graham Tchividjian

There is not a single thing that
Jesus cannot change, control, and conquer
because He is the living Lord.

Franklin Graham

God Is Love

This is what real love is: It is not our love for God; it is God's love for us in sending his Son to be the way to take away our sins.

1 John 4:10 NCV

The Bible makes this promise: God is love. It's a big promise, a very important description of who God is and how God works. God's love is perfect. When we open our hearts to His love, we are blessed and we are protected.

Today, offer sincere prayers of thanksgiving to your Heavenly Father. He loves you now and throughout all eternity. Open your heart to His presence and His love.

Today's Tip

God's love makes everything look a lot better. When you invite the love of God into your heart, everything in the world looks different, including you.

The Best Excuse Is No Excuse

Now the one who plants and the one who waters are equal, and each will receive his own reward according to his own labor.

1 Corinthians 3:8 HCSB

What is an excuse? Well, when you make up an excuse, that means that you try to come up with a good reason that you didn't do something that you should have done.

Anybody can make up excuses, and you can too. But you shouldn't get into the habit of making too many excuses. Why? Because excuses don't work. And why don't they work? Because everybody has already heard so many excuses that almost everybody can recognize excuses when they hear them.

So, the next time you're tempted to make up an excuse, don't. Instead of making an excuse, do what you think is right. After all, the very best excuse of all . . . is no excuse.

Sharing Your Stuff

It is more blessed to give than to receive.
Acts 20:35 HCSB

Are you one of those kids who is lucky enough to have a closet filled up with stuff? If so, it's probably time to share some of it.

When your mom or dad says it's time to clean up your closet and give some things away, don't be sad. Instead of whining, think about all the children who could enjoy the things that you don't use very much. And while you're at it, think about what Jesus might tell you to do if He were here. Jesus would tell you to share generously and cheerfully. And that's exactly what you should do!

Today's Tip

Your parents can help you find younger children who need the clothes and toys that you've outgrown.

Big Ideas About . . .

Self-Control

Here are two important ideas.
Take a few minutes to talk to your mom or dad
about what these quotations mean.

Your thoughts are the determining factor
as to whose mold you are conformed to.
Control your thoughts and you control
the direction of your life.

Charles Stanley

God nowhere tells us to give up things for
the sake of giving them up. He tells us to give
them up for the sake of the only thing worth
having—life with Himself.

Oswald Chambers

Think Before You Speak

To everything there is a season . . .
a time to keep silence, and a time to speak.
Ecclesiastes 3:1,7 KJV

Sometimes, it's easier to say the wrong thing than it is to say the right thing—especially if we're in a hurry to blurt out the first words that come into our heads. But, if we are patient and if we choose our words carefully, we can help other people feel better, and that's exactly what God wants us to do.

The Book of Proverbs tells us that the right words, spoken at the right time, can be wonderful gifts to our families and to our friends. That's why we should think about the things that we say before we say them, not after. When we do, our words make the world a better place, and that's exactly what God wants!

The Golden Rule Is Indeed Golden

Therefore, whatever you want others
to do for you, do also the same for them—
this is the Law and the Prophets.
Matthew 7:12 HCSB

The words of Matthew 7:12 remind us that,
as believers in Christ, we should treat others as
we wish to be treated. This is called the Golden
Rule, but for Christians, it's worth much more
than gold.

Do you want other people to forgive you
when you make mistakes? Of course, and that's
why you should be willing to forgive them.

The Golden Rule should be your tool for
deciding how you will treat others. So, use
the Golden Rule as your guide for living and
forgiving!

A Thought for Today

We are products of our past, but we don't
have to be prisoners of it. God specializes
in giving people a fresh start.
Rick Warren

Making Time for God

I wait quietly before God, for my hope is in him.
Psalm 62:5 NLT

When it comes to spending time with God, are you a "squeezer" or a "pleaser"? Do you squeeze God into your schedule with a prayer before mealtime, or do you please God by talking to Him far more often than that? If you're wise, you'll form the habit of spending time with God every day.

Even if you're the busiest kid on Planet Earth, you can still carve out a little time for God. And when you think about it, isn't that the very least you should do?

A Thought for Today

Growing in any area of the Christian life takes time, and the key is daily sitting at the feet of Jesus.
Cynthia Heald

Be Respectful

Show respect for all people.
Love the brothers and sisters of God's family.
1 Peter 2:17 ICB

Are you polite and respectful to your parents and teachers? And do you do your best to treat everybody with the respect they deserve? If you want to obey God's rules, then you should be able to answer yes to these questions.

Remember this: the Bible teaches you to be a respectful person—and if it's right there in the Bible, it's certainly the right thing to do!

Today's Tip

Calm down . . . sooner rather than later! If you're angry with your mom or your dad, don't blurt out something unkind. If you can't say anything nice, go to your room and don't come out until you can.

Big Ideas About . . .

What to Do
When Friends Misbehave

Here are two important ideas.
Take a few minutes to talk to your mom or dad
about what these quotations mean.

God has a plan for your friendships because
He knows your friends determine the quality
and direction of your life.

Charles Stanley

A friend is one
who makes me do my best.

Oswald Chambers

Sharing

If you have two shirts,
share with the person who does not have one.
If you have food, share that too.

Luke 3:11 ICB

How many times have you heard someone say, "Don't touch that; it's mine!" If you're like most of us, you've heard those words many times and you may have even said them yourself.

The Bible tells us that it's better for us to share things than it is to keep them all to ourselves. And the Bible also tells us that when we share, it's best to do so cheerfully. So today and every day, let's share. It's the best way because it's God's way.

Today's Tip

Your acts of kindness and generosity will speak far louder than words.

The Words You Speak

If anyone thinks he is religious, without controlling his tongue but deceiving his heart, his religion is useless.

James 1:26 HCSB

The words you speak are important. If you speak kind words, you make other people feel better. And that's exactly what you should do!

How hard is it to say a kind word? Not very! Yet, sometimes we're so busy that we forget to say the very things that might make other people feel better.

Kind words help; cruel words hurt. It's as simple as that. And, when we say the right thing at the right time, we give a gift that can change somebody's day or somebody's life.

Today's Tip

If you're not sure that it's the right thing to say, don't say it! And if you're not sure that it's the truth, don't tell it.

Today, Try to Memorize This Verse

I lift up my eyes to the hills—
where does my help come from?
My help comes from the LORD,
the Maker of heaven and earth.

Psalm 121:1-2 NIV

Here's a Bible verse that you should learn.
Practice saying it several times.
And then, talk to mom or dad
about exactly what the verse means.

The Rock

The Lord is my rock, my fortress, and my
deliverer, my God, my mountain where I seek
refuge. My shield, the horn of my salvation,
my stronghold, my refuge, and my Savior.

2 Samuel 22:2-3 HCSB

Life isn't always easy. Far from it!
Sometimes, life can be very hard indeed.
But even when we're upset or hurt, we must
remember that we're protected by a loving
Heavenly Father.

When we're worried, God can reassure us;
when we're sad, God can comfort us. When
our feelings are hurt, God is not just near, He
is here. We must lift our thoughts and prayers
to our Father in heaven. When we do, He will
answer our prayers. Why? Because He is our
shepherd, and He has promised to protect us
now and forever.

No More Tantrums

A patient person [shows] great understanding,
but a quick-tempered
one promotes foolishness.
Proverbs 14:29 HCSB

Temper tantrums are so silly. And so is pouting. So, of course, is whining. When we lose our tempers, we say things that we shouldn't say, and we do things that we shouldn't do. Too bad!

The Bible tells us that it is foolish to become angry and that it is wise to remain calm. That's why we should learn to control our tempers before our tempers control us.

Today's Tip

No more tantrums! If you think you're about to pitch a fit or throw a tantrum, slow down, catch your breath, and walk away if you must. It's better to walk away—and keep walking—than it is to blurt out angry words that can't be un-blurted.

Patience According to God

Patience is better than pride.
Ecclesiastes 7:8 NLT

God has a perfect idea of the kind of people He wants us to become. And for starters, He wants us to be loving, kind, and patient—not rude or mean!

The Bible tells us that God is love and that if we wish to know Him, we must have love in our hearts. Sometimes, of course, when we're tired, angry, or frustrated, it is very hard for us to be loving. Thankfully, anger and frustration are feelings that come and go, but God's love lasts forever.

If you'd like to become a more patient person, talk to God in prayer, listen to what He says, and share His love with your family and friends. God is always listening, and He's ready to talk to you . . . now!

Today's Tip

God has been patient with you . . . now it's your turn to be patient with others.

Know When to Say No

Wisdom will save you from
the ways of wicked men....

Proverbs 2:12 NIV

It happens to all of us at one time or
another: a friend asks us to do something that
we think is wrong. What should we do? Should
we try to please our friend by doing something
bad? No way! It's not worth it!

Trying to please our friends is okay. What's
not okay is misbehaving in order to do so.
Do you have a friend who encourages you
to misbehave? Hopefully, you don't have any
friends like that. But if you do, say "No, NO,
NOOOOOO!" And what if they threaten to
break up the friendship? Let them! Friendships
like that just aren't worth it.

A Thought for Today

Those who follow the crowd
usually get lost in it.

Rick Warren

Big Ideas About . . .

Cheerfulness

Here are two important ideas.
Take a few minutes to talk to your mom or dad
about what these quotations mean.

Cheerfulness strengthens
the heart and makes us try
harder to have a good life,
thus God's servants must always
be in good spirits.

St. Philip Neri

We may run, walk, stumble, drive, or fly,
but let us never lose sight of the reason for
the journey, or miss a chance to see
a rainbow on the way.

Gloria Gaither

This Crazy World

Do not love the world or the things
that belong to the world.
1 John 2:15 HCSB

An old hymn contains the words, "This
world is not my home; I'm just passing through."
Thank goodness! This crazy world can be a
place of trouble and danger. Thankfully, your
real home is heaven, a place where you can live
forever with Jesus.

In John 16:33, Jesus tells us He has
overcome the troubles of this world. We
should trust Him, and we should obey His
commandments. When we do, we are forever
blessed by the Son of God and His Father in
heaven.

Today's Tip

If you dwell on the world's message, you're
setting yourself up for disaster. If you dwell on
God's message, you're setting yourself up for
victory.

Are You Thankful?

Our prayers for you are always spilling over into
thanksgivings. We can't quit thanking God
our Father and Jesus our Messiah for you!

Colossians 1:3 MSG

Are you a thankful person? You should be!
Whether you realize it or not, you have much
to be thankful for. And who has given you
all the blessings you enjoy? Your parents are
responsible, of course. But all of our blessings
really start with God.

All of us should make thanksgiving a habit.
Since we have been given so much, the least we
can do is say "Thank You" to the One who has
given us more blessings than we can possibly
ever count.

Today's Tip

When is the best time to say "thanks" to God?
Any time. God loves you all the time, and that's
exactly why you should praise Him all the time.

If You're Trying to Be Perfect

You know the Lord is full of mercy and is kind.

James 5:11 NCV

If you're trying to be perfect, you're trying to do something that's impossible. No matter how much you try, you can't be a perfect person . . . and that's okay.

God doesn't expect you to live a mistake-free life—and neither should you. In the game of life, God expects you to try, but He doesn't always expect you to win. Sometimes, you'll make mistakes, but even then, you shouldn't give up!

So remember this: you don't have to be perfect to be a wonderful person. In fact, you don't even need to be "almost-perfect." You simply must try your best and leave the rest up to God.

Today's Tip

Don't be too hard on yourself: you don't have to be perfect to be wonderful.

Right and Wrong

Lead a tranquil and quiet life in
all godliness and dignity.

1 Timothy 2:2 HCSB

If you're old enough to know right from wrong, then you're old enough to do something about it. In other words, you should always try to do the right thing, and you should also do your very best not to do the wrong thing.

The more self-control you have, the easier it is to do the right thing. Why? Because, when you learn to think first and do things next, you avoid lots of silly mistakes. So here's great advice: first, slow down long enough to figure out the right thing to do—and then do it. You'll make yourself happy, and you'll make lots of other people happy, too.

Today's Tip

Good behavior leads to a happy life. And bad behavior doesn't. Behave accordingly.

The Love of Jesus

Just as the Father has loved Me,
I also have loved you. Remain in My love.
John 15:9 HCSB

The Bible makes this promise: Jesus loves you. And how should that make you feel? Well, the fact that Jesus loves you should make you very happy indeed, so happy, in fact, that you try your best to do the things that Jesus wants you to do.

Jesus wants you to welcome Him into your heart, He wants you to love and obey God, and He wants you to be kind to people. These are all very good things to do . . . and the rest is up to you!

Today's Tip

Jesus loves you so much that He gave His life so that you might live forever with Him in heaven. And how can you repay Christ's love? By accepting Him into your heart and by obeying His rules. When you do, He will love you and bless you always.

Setting An Example

We're Christ's representatives.
God uses us to persuade men and women
to drop their differences and enter into
God's work of making things right between
them. We're speaking for Christ himself now:
Become friends with God;
he's already a friend with you.
2 Corinthians 5:20 MSG

The Bible says that you are "the light that gives light to the world." The Bible also says that you should live in a way that lets other people understand what it means to be a good person. And of course, learning to share is an important part of being a good person.

What kind of "light" have you been giving off? Hopefully, you have been a good example for everybody to see. Why? Because the world needs all the light it can get, and that includes your light, too!

Today, Try to Memorize This Verse

The Lord is my shepherd;
I shall not want.

Psalm 23:1 KJV

Here's a Bible verse that you should learn.
Practice saying it several times.
And then, talk to mom or dad
about exactly what the verse means.

Feeling Better

A wise person is patient. He will be honored
if he ignores a wrong done against him.

Proverbs 19:11 ICB

Is forgiving someone else an easy thing for
you to do or a hard thing? If you're like most
people, forgiving others can be hard, Hard,
HARD! But even if you're having a very hard
time forgiving someone, you can do it if you
talk things over with your parents, and if you
talk things over with God.

Do you find forgiveness difficult? Talk
about it and pray about it. You'll feel better
when you do.

A Thought for Today

When God forgives, He forgets. He buries our
sins in the sea and puts a sign on the shore
saying, "No Fishing Allowed."

Corrie ten Boom

Solomon Says ... Be Kind!

Therefore, God's chosen ones, holy and loved, put on heartfelt compassion, kindness, humility, gentleness, and patience.

Colossians 3:12 HCSB

King Solomon wrote most of the Book of Proverbs; in it, he gave us wonderful advice for living wisely. Solomon warned that unkind behavior leads only to trouble, but kindness is its own reward.

The next time you're tempted to say an unkind word, remember Solomon. He was one of the wisest men who ever lived, and he knew that it's always better to be kind. And now, you know it, too.

Today's Tip

Remember, the Golden Rule starts with you!

Share Your Love

God is love, and the one who remains in love
remains in God, and God remains in him.
1 John 4:16 HCSB

The Bible tells us that God is love and that
if we wish to know Him, we must have love in
our hearts. Sometimes, of course, when we're
tired, angry, or frustrated, it is very hard for us
to be loving. Thankfully, anger and frustration
are feelings that come and go, but God's love
lasts forever.

If you'd like to improve your day and your
life, share God's love with your family and
friends. Every time you love, and every time you
give, God smiles.

A Thought for Today

When God scooped out the valleys and created
the mountains, when He hung the stars and
blew the wind, you were on His mind.

Steve Brown

God Has a Plan

We can make our plans, but the LORD
determines our steps.

Proverbs 16:9 NLT

God has a plan for you. But God's plan may
not always happen in the way that you would
like or at the time of your own choosing. Still,
God always knows best.

Sometimes, even though you may want
something very badly, you must still be patient
and wait for the right time to get it, And the
right time, of course, is determined by God. So
trust Him always, obey Him always, and wait for
Him to show you His plans. And that's exactly
what He will do.

Today's Tip

Whose plans will you trust, yours or God's? The
answer should be obvious. So ,as you plan for
this day and for all the ones that follow it, plan
carefully and prayerfully.

Respecting Others

Just as you want others to do for you,
do the same for them.

Luke 6:31 HCSB

How should you treat other people? Jesus has the answer to that question. Jesus wants you to treat other people exactly like you want to be treated: with kindness, respect, and courtesy. When you do, you'll make your family and friends happy . . . and that's what God wants.

So, if you're wondering how to treat someone else, follow the Golden Rule: treat other people like you want them to treat you. When you do, you'll be obeying your Father in heaven and you'll be making other folks happy at the same time.

Today's Tip

When dealing with other people, it is important to try to "walk in their shoes."

Big Ideas About . . .

What Happens When You Pray

Here are two important ideas.
Take a few minutes to talk to your mom or dad
about what these quotations mean.

Prayer accomplishes more than anything else.

Bill Bright

Prayer succeeds when all else fails.

E. M. Bounds

Doing The Right Thing

The honest person will live safely,
but the one who is dishonest will be caught.
Proverbs 10:9 ICB

Nobody can tell the truth for you. You're the one who decides what you are going to say. You're the one who decides whether your words will be truthful . . . or not.

The word "integrity" means doing the right and honest thing. If you're going to be a person of integrity, it's up to you. If you want to live a life that is pleasing to God and to others, make integrity a habit. When you do, everybody wins, especially you!

Today's Tip

Honesty, Honesty, Honesty! Unless you build your relationships on honesty, you're building on a slippery, sandy slope.

Getting to Know God

If your life honors the name of Jesus,
he will honor you.

2 Thessalonians 1:12 MSG

There's really no way around it: If you want
to know God, you need to know His Son. And
that's good, because getting to know Jesus
can—and should—be a wonderful experience.

Jesus has an amazing love for you, so
welcome Him into your heart today. When you
do, you'll always be grateful that you did.

Today's Tip

Do you want them to follow in the footsteps
of Jesus? Then you must lead the way. Actions
speak louder than sermons . . . much louder.

Kindness Starts with You

Don't pick on people, jump on their failures, criticize their faults—unless, of course, you want the same treatment. Don't condemn those who are down; that hardness can boomerang. Be easy on people; you'll find life a lot easier.
Luke 6:36-37 MSG

If you're waiting for other people to be nice to you before you're nice to them, you've got it backwards. Kindness starts with you! You see, you can never control what other people will say or do, but you can control your own behavior.

The Bible tells us that we should never stop doing good deeds as long as we live. Kindness is God's way, and it should be our way, too.

A Thought for Today

It doesn't take monumental feats to make the world a better place. It can be as simple as letting someone go ahead of you in a grocery line.
Barbara Johnson

Your Family Is a Gift

Their first responsibility is to show godliness at
home and repay their parents by taking
care of them. This is something that
pleases God very much.

1 Timothy 5:4 NLT

Your family is a wonderful, one-of-a-kind
gift from God. And your family members love
you very much—what a blessing it is to be
loved!

Have you ever really stopped to think about
how much you are loved? Your parents love you
(of course) and so does everybody else in your
family. But it doesn't stop there. You're also an
important part of God's family . . . and He loves
you more than you can imagine.

What should you do about all the love that
comes your way? You should accept it; you
should be thankful for it; and you should share
it . . . starting now!

Everybody Makes Mistakes

If you hide your sins, you will not succeed.
If you confess and reject them,
you will receive mercy.
Proverbs 28:13 NCV

Do you make mistakes? Of course you do . . . everybody does. When you make a mistake, you must try your best to learn from it so that you won't make the very same mistake again. And, if you have hurt someone—or if you have disobeyed God—you must ask for forgiveness.

Remember: mistakes are a part of life, but the biggest mistake you can make is to keep making the same mistake over and over and over again.

Today's Tip

Fix it sooner rather than later: If you make a mistake, the time to make things better is now, not later! The sooner you admit your mistake, the better.

Obeying God

But be doers of the word and not hearers only.
James 1:22 HCSB

How can you show God how much you love Him? By obeying His commandments, that's how! When you follow God's rules, you show Him that you have real respect for Him and for His Son.

Sometimes, you will be tempted to disobey God, but don't do it. And sometimes you'll be tempted to disobey your parents or your teachers . . . but don't do that, either.

When your parent steps away or a teacher looks away, it's up to you to control yourself. And of this you can be sure: If you really want to control yourself, you can do it!

Today's Tip

Associate with friends who, by their words and actions, encourage you to obey God.

Becoming a More Patient Person

Be gentle to all, able to teach, patient.

2 Timothy 2:24 NKJV

The Book of Proverbs tells us that patience is a very good thing. But for most of us, patience can also be a very hard thing. After all, we have many things that we want, and we want them NOW! But the Bible tells us that we must learn to wait patiently for the things that God has in store for us.

Are you having trouble being patient? If so, remember that patience takes practice, and lots of it, so keep trying. And if you make a mistake, don't be too upset. After all, if you're going to be a really patient person, you shouldn't just be patient with others, you should also be patient with yourself.

Today's Tip

An important part of growing up is learning to be patient with others and with yourself. And one more thing: learn from everybody's mistakes, especially your own.

Don't Copy Friends Who Misbehave

Stay away from a foolish man;
you will gain no knowledge from his speech.
Proverbs 14:7 HCSB

If your friends misbehave, do you misbehave right along with them, or do you tell them to stop? Usually, it's much easier to go along with your friends, even if you know they're misbehaving. But it's always better to do the right thing, even if it's hard.

Sometimes, grownups must stand up for the things they believe in. When they do, it can be hard for them, too. But the Bible tells us over and over again that we should do the right thing, not the easy thing.

When your friends misbehave, it can spoil everything. So if your friends behave badly, don't copy them! And if your friends keep behaving badly, choose different friends.

A Thought for Today

Comparison is the root of
all feelings of inferiority.
James Dobson

Kind Thoughts

Whoever forgives someone's sin
makes a friend, but gossiping about
the sin breaks up friendships.
Proverbs 17:9 NCV

What does it mean to forgive? Forgiveness
means that you decide to change your angry
thoughts into kind thoughts. Forgiveness means
that you decide not to stay mad at somebody
who has done something wrong. Forgiveness
happens when you decide that obeying God is
more important than staying angry.

Sometimes forgiveness can be very hard,
but it's the right thing to do. Why? Because
forgiveness is God's way, and you should make
it your way, too!

A Thought for Today

We cannot be right with God until
we are right with one another.
Charles Swindoll

He Answers

The intense prayer of the righteous
is very powerful.
James 5:16 HCSB

In case you've been wondering, wonder no more—God does answer your prayers. What God does not do is this: He does not always answer your prayers as soon as you might like, and He does not always answer your prayers by saying "Yes."

God answers prayers not only according to our wishes but also according to His master plan. And guess what? We don't know that plan . . . but we can know the Planner.

Are you praying? Then you can be sure that God is listening. And sometime soon, He'll answer!

A Thought for Today

You don't need fancy words or religious phrases. Just tell God the way it really is.

Jim Cymbala

Respect for Others

Being respected is more important
than having great riches.

Proverbs 22:1 ICB

Do you try to have a respectful attitude towards everybody? Hopefully so!

Should you be respectful of grown ups? Of course. Teachers? Certainly. Family members? Yes. Friends? Yep, but it doesn't stop there. The Bible teaches us to treat all people with respect.

Respect for others is habit-forming: the more you do it, the easier it becomes. So start practicing right now. Say lots of kind words and do lots of kind things, because when it comes to kindness and respect, practice makes perfect.

Today's Tip

How did Jesus treat the people who lived on the edges of society? With patience, respect, and love.

A Great Big Thank You

Praise the LORD. Give thanks to the LORD,
for he is good; his love endures forever.
Psalm 106:1 NIV

If you're like most kids, you're very busy
doing things and learning things. But no matter
how busy you are—even if you hardly have a
moment to spare—you should still slow down
and say "Thank You," to God!.

God has given you many things, and you
owe Him everything, including a GREAT BIG
THANK YOU, starting now (and ending never!)

Today's Tip

In good times or difficult times, it is important
to understand the need to praise God.

Is the Golden Rule Your Rule, Too?

Don't be obsessed with getting your own advantage. Forget yourselves long enough to lend a helping hand.

Philippians 2:4 MSG

Is the Golden Rule your rule, or is it just another Bible verse that goes in one ear and out the other? Jesus made Himself perfectly clear: He instructed you to treat other people in the same way that you want to be treated. But sometimes, especially when you're feeling pressure from friends, or when we're tired or upset, obeying the Golden Rule can seem like an impossible task—but it's not. So be kind to everybody and obey God's rule, the Golden Rule, that is.

Today's Tip

In order to be a good person, you must do good things. So get busy! The best time to do a good deed is as soon as you can do it!

Mistakes: Nobody Likes 'Em

Therefore, if anyone is in Christ,
he is a new creation; the old has gone,
the new has come!

2 Corinthians 5:17 NIV

Mistakes: nobody likes 'em but everybody makes 'em. And you're no different! When you make mistakes (and you will), you should do your best to correct them, to learn from them, and pray for the wisdom to avoid those same mistakes in the future.

If you want to become smarter faster, you'll learn from your mistakes the first time you make them. When you do, that means that you won't keep making the same mistakes over and over again, and that's the smart way to live.

Today's Tip

Made a mistake? Ask for forgiveness! If you've broken one of God's rules, you can always ask Him for His forgiveness. And He will always give it!

Parents Can Help

God-loyal people, living honest lives,
make it much easier for their children.
Proverbs 20:7 MSG

Whenever you want to get better at something, you should always be willing to let your parents help out in any way they can. After all, your parents want you to become the very best person you can be. So, if you want to become better at controlling your own behavior, ask your parents to help. How can they help out? By reminding you to slow down and think about things before you do them—not after. It's as simple as that.

Today's Tip

Your parents love you and want to help you. Their job is to help . . . your job is to listen carefully to the things they say.

Big Ideas About . . .

Heaven

Here are two important ideas.
Take a few minutes to talk to your mom or dad
about what these quotations mean.

What joy that the Bible tells us
the great comfort that the best
is yet to be. Our outlook goes
beyond this world.

Corrie ten Boom

Earth's best is only a dim reflection
and a preliminary rendering of the glory
that will one day be revealed.

Joni Eareckson Tada

You Can't Please Everybody

My son, if sinners entice you,
don't be persuaded.
Proverbs 1:10 HCSB

Are you one of those people who tries to please everybody in sight? If so, you'd better watch out! After all, if you worry too much about pleasing your friends, you may not worry enough about pleasing God.

Who will you try to please today: your God or your pals? The answer to that question should be simple. Your first job is to obey God's rules . . . and that means obeying your parents, too!

So don't worry too much about pleasing your friends or neighbors. Try, instead, to please your heavenly Father and your parents. No exceptions.

Today's Tip

You simply cannot please everybody. So here's what you should do: Try pleasing God and your parents.

Practicing Forgiveness

Smart people know how to hold their tongue;
their grandeur is to forgive and forget.
Proverbs 19:11 MSG

Forgiving other people requires practice
and lots of it. So when it comes to forgiveness,
here's something you should remember: if at
first you don't succeed, don't give up!

Are you having trouble forgiving someone
(or, for that matter, forgiving yourself for a
mistake that you've made)? If so, remember
that forgiveness isn't easy, so keep trying until
you get it right . . . and if you keep trying, you
can be sure that sooner or later, you will get it
right.

Today's Tip

For most of us—kids and grown-ups alike—
forgiveness doesn't come naturally. Keep
practicing until it does.

Today, Try to Memorize This Verse

Those who hope in the LORD
will renew their strength.
They will soar on wings like eagles;
they will run and not grow weary,
they will walk and not be faint.

Isaiah 40:31 NIV

Here's a Bible verse that you should learn.
Practice saying it several times.
And then, talk to mom or dad
about exactly what the verse means.

Be the Right Kind of Christian

Let us live in a right way . . . clothe yourselves
with the Lord Jesus Christ and forget about
satisfying your sinful self.

Romans 13:13-14 NCV

Do you want to be the kind of Christian
that God intends for you to be? It's up to you!
You'll be the one who will decide how you
behave.

If you decide to obey God and trust His
Son, you will be rewarded now and forever.
So guard your heart and trust your heavenly
Father. He will never lead you astray.

Today's Tip

It's easy to blame others when you get into
trouble . . . but it's wrong. Instead of trying to
blame other people for your own misbehavior,
take responsibility . . . and learn from your
mistakes!

Peace According to God

I leave you peace. My peace I give you.
I do not give it to you as the world does.
So don't let your hearts be troubled.
John 14:27 ICB

The words from John 14:27 remind us that Jesus offers us peace, not as the world gives, but as He alone gives. We, as believers, can accept His peace or ignore it. When we accept the peace of Jesus Christ into our hearts, our lives are changed forever, and we become more loving, patient Christians.

Christ's peace is offered freely; it has already been paid for; it is ours for the asking. So let us ask . . . and then share.

A Thought for Today

You're in a hurry. God is not. Trust God.
Marie T. Freeman

Do Good Deeds

A good person produces good deeds from
a good heart, and an evil person produces evil
deeds from an evil heart. Whatever is in
your heart determines what you say.

Luke 6:45 NLT

It's good to do good deeds. Even when
nobody's watching, God is. And God knows
whether you've done the right thing or the
wrong thing.

So if you're tempted to misbehave when
nobody is looking, remember this: There
is never a time when "nobody's watching."
Somebody is always watching over you—and
that Somebody, of course, is your Father in
Heaven. Don't let Him down!

Today's Tip

Goodness is as goodness does: In order to be a
good person, you must do good things. Thinking
about them isn't enough. So get busy! Your
family and friends need all the good deeds they
can get!

Big Ideas About . . .

God's Love

Here are two important ideas.
Take a few minutes to talk to your mom or dad
about what these quotations mean.

The Bible has a simple story.
God made man.
Man rejected God.
God won't give up
until he wins him back.

Max Lucado

The love of God is revealed in that He
laid down His life for His enemies.

Oswald Chambers

The Very Best Time to Forgive Somebody Is Now

If someone does wrong to you,
do not pay him back by doing wrong to him.
Romans 12:17 ICB

When is the best time to forgive somebody? Well, as the old saying goes, there's no time like the present. So, if you have somebody you need to forgive, why not forgive that person today?

Forgiving other people is one of the ways that we make ourselves feel better. So, if you're still angry about something that somebody did, forgive that person right now. There is no better time.

Today's Tip

When the Lord tells you it is time to do something (like forgive someone), the time to do it is now.

Today, Try to Memorize This Verse

Everything is possible to the one who believes.

Mark 9:23 HCSB

Here's a Bible verse that you should learn.
Practice saying it several times.
And then, talk to mom or dad
about exactly what the verse means.

Yes, Jesus Loves You!

A devout life does bring wealth, but it's the rich simplicity of being yourself before God.

1 Timothy 6:6 MSG

Have you heard the song "Jesus Loves Me?" Probably so. It's a happy song that should remind you of this important fact: Jesus loves you very much.

When you invite Jesus into your heart, He will be your friend forever. If you make mistakes, He'll still be your friend. When you aren't perfect, He'll still love you. If you feel sorry or sad, He can help you feel better.

Yes, Jesus loves you . . . and you should love yourself. So the next time you feel sad about yourself . . . or something that you've done . . . remember that Jesus loves you, your family loves you, and you should feel that way, too.

Today's Tip

Nobody else in the world is exactly like you. When God made you, He made a very special, one-of-a-kind person. So don't forget this fact: you're very, very, very, very, very special.

Friends Should Share

Dear friend, you are showing your faith by
whatever you do for the brothers,
and this you are doing for strangers.

3 John 1:5 HCSB

How can you be a good friend? One way is
by sharing. And here are some of the things
you can share: smiles, kind words, pats on the
back, your toys, school supplies, books, and, of
course, your prayers.

Would you like to make your friends happy?
And would you like to make yourself happy at
the same time? Here's how: treat your friends
like you want to be treated. That means
obeying the Golden Rule, which, of course,
means sharing. In fact, the more you share, the
better friend you'll be.

Today's Tip

Sharing with guests is an important way to
demonstrate hospitality.

Mary and Martha

But Martha was pulled away by all she had
to do in the kitchen. Later, she stepped in,
interrupting them. "Master, don't you care that
my sister has abandoned the kitchen to me?
Tell her to lend me a hand." The Master said,
"Martha, dear Martha, you're fussing far too
much and getting yourself worked up
over nothing. One thing only is essential,
and Mary has chosen it—it's the main course,
and won't be taken from her."

Luke 10:40-42 MSG

Okay, after that rather long Bible passage,
your devotional is almost up, so we'll make it
short and sweet: Martha was concerned with
doing things for Jesus. Mary was concerned
with being with Jesus. Mary made the better
choice. Why? Because we need to be with
Christ before we start doing things for Him.
End of lesson.

The Habit Of Honesty

Those who want to do right more than anything
else are happy. God will fully satisfy them.

Matthew 5:6 ICB

Our lives are made up of lots and lots
of habits. And the habits we choose help
determine the kind of people we become. If we
choose habits that are good, we are happier
and healthier. If we choose habits that are
bad, then it's too bad for us!

Honesty, like so many other things, is a
habit. And it's a habit that is right for you.

Do you want to grow up to become the
kind of person that God intends for you to be?
Then get into the habit of being honest with
everybody. You'll be glad you did . . . and so will
God!

A Thought for Today

If you want to form a new habit,
get to work. If you want to break a bad habit,
get on your knees.

Marie T. Freeman

White Lies?

Doing what is right brings freedom
to honest people.

Proverbs 11:6 ICB

Sometimes, people convince themselves that it's okay to tell "little white lies." Sometimes people convince themselves that itsy bitsy lies aren't harmful. But there's a problem: little lies have a way of growing into big ones, and once they grow up, they cause lots of problems.

Remember that lies, no matter what size, are not part of God's plan for our lives, so tell the truth about everything. It's the right thing to do, and besides: when you always tell the truth, you don't have to try and remember what you said!

A Thought for Today

The single most important element in any human relationship is honesty—with oneself, with God, and with others.

Catherine Marshall

A Fruitful Friendship

I am the Vine, you are the branches.
When you're joined with me and I with you,
the relation intimate and organic,
the harvest is sure to be abundant.

John 15:5 MSG

Whether you realize it or not, you already have a relationship with Jesus. Hopefully, it's a close relationship! Why? Because the friendship you form with Jesus will help you every day of your life . . . and beyond!

You can either choose to invite Him into your heart, or you can ignore Him altogether. Welcome Him today—and while you're at it, encourage your friends and family members to do the same.

A Thought for Today

I am truly happy with Jesus Christ.
I couldn't live without Him. When my life gets
beyond the ability to cope, He takes over.

Ruth Bell Graham

Laughter Is a Gift

There is a time for everything, and everything
on earth has its special season.
There is a time to cry and a time to laugh.
There is a time to be sad and a time to dance.

Ecclesiastes 3:1,4 NCV

Do you like to laugh? Of course you do!
Laughter is a gift from God that He hopes
you'll use in the right way. So here are a few
things to remember:

1. God wants you to be happy. 2. Laughter is
a good thing when you're laughing at the right
things. 3. You should laugh with people, but you
should never laugh at them.

God created laughter for a reason...and
God knows best. So do yourself a favor: laugh
at the right things . . . and laugh a lot!

Today's Tip

Learn to laugh at life. Life has a lighter side—
look for it, especially when times are tough.
Laughter is medicine for the soul, so take your
medicine early and often.

Big Ideas About . . .

Going to Church

Here are two important ideas.
Take a few minutes to talk to your mom or dad
about what these quotations mean.

The church needs people
who are doers of the Word
and not just hearers.

Warren Wiersbe

The Bible knows nothing of
solitary religion.

John Wesley

Obey Your Teachers

Likewise you younger people,
submit yourselves to your elders.
1 Peter 5:5 NKJV

It's good to obey your teachers, but before you can obey them, you must make sure you understand what your teachers are saying. So, in order to be an obedient student, you must be a student who knows how to listen.

Once you decide to be a careful listener, you'll become a better learner, too. But if you're determined to talk to other kids while your teachers are teaching, you won't learn very much.

So do yourself a favor: when you go to school, listen and obey. You'll be glad you did . . . and your teachers will be glad, too.

Today's Tip

Learning how to obey makes you a better person. You have many teachers. Listen to them and obey them. When you do, you'll become a better person.

Be Hopeful!

Make me hear joy and gladness.
Psalm 51:8 NKJV

Hope is a very good thing to have . . . and to share. So make this promise to yourself and keep it: promise yourself that you'll be a hopeful person. Think good thoughts. Trust God. Become friends with Jesus. And trust your hopes, not your fears. Then, when you've filled your heart with hope and gladness, share your good thoughts with friends. They'll be better for it, and so will you.

Today's Tip

Think about all the things you have (starting with your family and your faith) . . . and think about all the things you can do! Believe in yourself.

Today, Try to Memorize This Verse

Now these three remain:
faith, hope, and love.
But the greatest of these
is love.

1 Corinthians 13:13 HCSB

Here's a Bible verse that you should learn.
Practice saying it several times.
And then, talk to mom or dad
about exactly what the verse means.

Think About the Other Person

I pray that your love for each other
will overflow more and more, and that
you will keep on growing in
your knowledge and understanding.

Philippians 1:9 NLT

There's an old saying that goes something like this: "Try to put yourself in the other person's shoes." It means that the more you understand somebody, the easier it is to forgive that person.

When you become angry with someone, try putting yourself in the other person's shoes. When you do, perhaps you'll be a little bit more understanding—and a little bit quicker to forgive.

A Thought for Today

When you extend hospitality to others, you're not trying to impress people; you're trying to reflect God to them.

Max Lucado

About Barnabas

Barnabas was a good man,
full of the Holy Spirit and full of faith.
Acts 11:23-24 ICB

Barnabas was a leader in the early Christian church who was known for his kindness and for his ability to encourage others. Because of Barnabas, many people were introduced to Christ.

We become like Barnabas when we speak kind words to our families and to our friends. And then, because we have been generous and kind, the people around us can see how Christians should behave. So when in doubt, be kind and generous to others, just like Barnabas.

Today's Tip

Be an encourager! Barnabas was known as a man who encouraged others. In other words, he made other people feel better by saying kind things. You, like Barnabas, can encourage your family and friends . . . and you should.

Avoiding Mischief

Therefore as you have received Christ Jesus
the Lord, walk in Him.
Colossians 2:6 HCSB

Face facts: not everybody you know is well
behaved. Your first job is to recognize bad
behavior when you see it . . . and your second
job is to make sure that you don't join in!

The moment that you decide to avoid
mischief whenever you see it is the moment
that you'll make yourself happy, your parents
happy, and God happy. And you'll stay out of
trouble. And you'll be glad you did!

A Thought for Today

Christians are the citizens of heaven,
and while we are on earth,
we ought to behave like heaven's citizens.
Warren Wiersbe

Today, Try to Memorize This Verse

And remember,
I am with you always,
to the end of the age.

Matthew 28:20 HCSB

Here's a Bible verse that you should learn.
Practice saying it several times.
And then, talk to mom or dad
about exactly what the verse means.

Solomon: A Very Wise Man

*If you need wisdom—if you want to know
what God wants you to do—ask him,
and he will gladly tell you.
He will not resent your asking.*

James 1:5 NLT

Solomon wasn't just a king. He was also a very wise man and a very good writer. He even wrote several books in the Bible! So when He finally put down His pen, what was this wise man's final advice? It's simple: Solomon said: "Honor God and obey His commandments."

The next time you have an important choice to make, ask yourself this: "Am I honoring God and obeying Him? And am I doing what God wants me to do?" If you can answer those questions with a great big "YES," then go ahead. But if you're uncertain if the choice you are about to make is the right one, slow down. Why? Because that's what Solomon says . . . and that's what God says, too!

Working Together

Work at getting along with each other
and with God. Otherwise you'll never get
so much as a glimpse of God.

Hebrews 12:14 MSG

Helping other people can be fun! When you
help others, you feel better about yourself—
and you'll know that God approves of what
you're doing.

When you learn how to cooperate with your
family and friends, you'll soon discover that it's
more fun when everybody works together.

So do everybody a favor: learn better ways
to share and better ways to cooperate. It's the
right thing to do.

Today's Tip

Cooperation pays. When you cooperate with
your friends and family, you'll feel good about
yourself—and your family and friends will feel
good about you, too.

Big Ideas About . . .

God's Gifts

Here are two important ideas.
Take a few minutes to talk to your mom or dad
about what these quotations mean.

God gives His gifts where He
finds the vessel empty enough
to receive them.

C. S. Lewis

God is the giver, and we are the receivers.
And His richest gifts are bestowed
not upon those who do the greatest things,
but upon those who accept
His abundance and His grace.

Hannah Whitall Smith

What Kind Of Example?

You are young, but do not let anyone treat you as if you were not important. Be an example to show the believers how they should live. Show them with your words, with the way you live, with your love, with your faith, and with your pure life.

1 Timothy 4:12 ICB

Like it or not, your behavior is a powerful example to others. The question is not whether you will be an example to your friends; the only question is this: What kind of example will you be?

Corrie ten Boom advised, "Don't worry about what you do not understand. Worry about what you do understand in the Bible but do not live by." And that's good advice because your family and friends are always watching . . . and so, for that matter, is God.

A Thought for Today

Be careful how you live. You may be the only Bible some person ever reads.

William J. Toms

Obeying God

Pay all your debts, except the debt of love for
others. You can never finish paying that!
If you love your neighbor, you will fulfill
all the requirements of God's law.

Romans 13:8 NLT

How hard is it to forgive people? Sometimes,
it's very hard! But God tells us that we must
forgive other people, even when we'd rather
not forgive them. So, if you're angry with
anybody (or if you're upset by something you
yourself have done) it's time to forgive.

God instructs us to treat other people
exactly as we wish to be treated. When we
forgive others, we are obeying our Heavenly
Father, and that's exactly what we must try to
do.

Today's Tip

Forgiving other people is not necessarily the
same as forgetting. Yet even when you cannot
forget the past, you should try not to focus on
the past.

Real Friends

A friend loves you all the time.
Proverbs 17:17 ICB

The Book of Proverbs tells us that true friends love us always. How wonderful that is! We should thank God for the family and friends He has brought into our lives.

Today, let's give thanks to God for all the people who love us, for brothers and sisters, parents and grandparents, aunts and uncles, cousins, and friends. And then, as a way of thanking God, let's obey Him by being especially kind to our loved ones. They deserve it, and so does He.

Today's Tip

To grow your friendships, make the effort to spend time with your friends.

Sharing And Self-esteem

God loves the person who gives happily.
2 Corinthians 9:7 ICB

Learning how to share can be an important way to build better self-esteem. Why? Because when you learn to share your things, you'll know that you've done exactly what God wants you to do—and you'll feel better about yourself.

The Bible teaches that it's better to be generous than selfish. But sometimes, you won't feel like sharing your things, and you'll be tempted to keep everything for yourself. When you're feeling a little bit stingy, remember this: God wants you to share your things with people who need your help.

When you learn to be a more generous person, God will be pleased with you . . . and you'll be pleased with yourself.

Today's Tip

Some of the best stuff you'll ever have is the stuff you give away.

Difficult Days

We take the good days from God—
why not also the bad days?
Job 2:10 MSG

Face it: some days are better than others.
But even on the days when you don't feel very
good, God never leaves you for even a moment.
So if you need assistance, you can always pray
to God, knowing that He will listen and help.

If you're feeling unhappy, talk things over
with God, and while you're at it, be sure and
talk things over with your parents, too. And
remember this: the sooner you start talking, the
sooner things will get better.

A Thought for Today

When life is difficult, God wants us to have
a faith that trusts and waits.

Kay Arthur

God's Power

But Jesus looked at them and said,
"With men this is impossible,
but with God all things are possible."
Matthew 19:26 HCSB

How strong is God? Stronger than anybody can imagine! But even if we can't understand God's power, we can respect His power. And we can be sure that God has the strength to guide us and protect us forever.

The next time you're worried or afraid, remember this: if God is powerful enough to create the universe and everything in it, He's also strong enough to take care of you. Now that's a comforting thought!

A Thought for Today

The power of God through His Spirit will work within us to the degree that we permit it.
Mrs. Charles E. Cowman

Big Ideas About...

Obedience

Here are two important ideas.
Take a few minutes to talk to your mom or dad
about what these quotations mean.

You may not always see
immediate results,
but all God wants is your
obedience and faithfulness.

Vonette Bright

The surest evidence of our love to Christ is
obedience to the laws of Christ.
Love is the root, obedience is the fruit.

Matthew Henry

Staying Out of Trouble

Don't envy bad people; don't even want
to be around them. All they think about
is causing a disturbance;
all they talk about is making trouble.

Proverbs 24:1-2 MSG

One way that you can feel better about
yourself is by staying out of trouble. And one
way that you can stay out of trouble is by
making friends with people who, like you, want
to do what's right.

Are your friends the kind of kids who
encourage you to behave yourself? If so, you've
chosen your friends wisely. But if your friends
try to get you in trouble, perhaps it's time to
think long and hard about making some new
friends.

Whether you know it or not, you're probably
going to behave like your friends behave. So
pick out friends who make you want to behave
better, not worse. When you do, you'll feel
better about yourself . . . a whole lot better.

Sometimes It's Hard to be Honest ... But It's Always Right

It is better to be poor and honest
than to be foolish and tell lies.
Proverbs 19:1 ICB

Telling the truth can be hard sometimes. But even when telling the truth is very hard, that's exactly what you should do. If you're afraid to tell the truth, pray to God for the courage to do the right thing, and then do it!

If you've ever told a big lie, and then had to live with the big consequences of that lie, you know that it's far more trouble to tell a lie than it is to tell the truth. But lies aren't just troubling to us; they're also troubling to God! So tell the truth, even when it's hard to do; you'll be glad you did . . . and so will He!

A Thought for Today

A lie is like a snowball: the further you roll it,
the bigger it becomes.
Martin Luther

The Master Teacher

This man came to Him at night and said,
"Rabbi, we know that You have come from God
as a teacher, for no one could perform these
signs You do unless God were with him."

John 3:2 HCSB

Who was the greatest teacher in the history
of the world? Jesus was . . and He still is! Jesus
teaches us how to live, how to behave, and
how to worship. Now, it's up to each of us, as
Christians, to learn the important lessons that
Jesus can teach.

Some day soon, you will have learned
everything that Jesus has to teach you, right?
WRONG!!!! Jesus will keep teaching you
important lessons throughout your life. And
that's good, because all of us, kids and grown-
ups alike, have lots to learn . . . especially from
the Master . . . and the Master, of course, is
Jesus.

It's Important to Be Kind

I tell you the truth,
anything you did for even the least
of my people here, you also did for me.

Matthew 25:40 NCV

The Bible promises that if you're a nice person, good things will happen to you. That's one reason (but not the only reason) that it's important to be kind.

Do you listen to your heart when it tells you to be kind to other people? Hopefully, you do. After all, lots of people in the world aren't as fortunate as you are—and some of these folks are living very near you.

Ask your parents to help you find ways to do nice things for other people. And don't forget that everybody needs love, kindness, and respect, so you should always be ready to share those things, too.

Big Ideas About . . .

Too Much Stuff

Here are two important ideas.
Take a few minutes to talk to your mom or dad
about what these quotations mean.

If you want to be truly happy,
you won't find it on an endless quest for
more stuff. You'll find it in receiving
God's generosity and then passing
that generosity along.

Bill Hybels

There is absolutely no evidence that
complexity and materialism lead to happiness.
On the contrary, there is plenty of evidence
that simplicity and spirituality lead to joy,
a blessedness that is better than happiness.

Dennis Swanberg

Obey and Forgive

This is love for God: to obey his commands.
1 John 5:3 NIV

We know that it's right to forgive other people and wrong to stay angry with them. But sometimes, it's so much easier to do the wrong thing than it is to do the right thing, especially when we're tired or frustrated.

When you do the right thing by forgiving other people, you'll feel good because you'll know that you're obeying God. And that's a very good feeling indeed. So make this promise to yourself and keep it: play by the rules—God's rules. You'll always be glad you did.

Today's Tip

Your obedience to God is a demonstration of the gratitude that you feel in your heart for the blessings you have been given.

How Much Is Too Much?

Since we entered the world penniless and will
leave it penniless, if we have bread on the table
and shoes on our feet, that's enough.

1 Timothy 6:7-8 MSG

How much stuff is too much stuff? Well,
if your desire for stuff is getting in the way of
your desire to know God, then you've got too
much stuff—it's as simple as that.

If you find yourself worrying too much
about stuff, it's time to change the way you
think about the things you own. Stuff isn't
really very important to God, and it shouldn't
be too important to you.

Today's Tip

The world wants you to believe that "money
and stuff" can buy happiness. Don't believe it!
Genuine happiness comes not from money, but
from the things that money can't buy—starting,
of course, with your relationship to God and
His only begotten Son.

Lost in the Crowd?

We must obey God rather than men.
Acts 5:29 NASB

Rick Warren observed, "Those who follow the crowd usually get lost in it." We know those words to be true, but oftentimes we fail to live by them. Instead of trusting God for guidance, we imitate our friends and suffer the consequences.

Instead of getting lost in the crowd, you should find guidance from your parents and from God. When you do, you'll be happier . . . much happier!

Today's Tip

Being obedient to God means that you cannot always please other people.

Keep Your Cool

Work hard, but not just to please your masters
when they are watching. As slaves of Christ,
do the will of God with all your heart.
Work with enthusiasm, as though you were
working for the Lord rather than for people.

Ephesians 6:6-7 NLT

If you've lost patience with someone, or if
you're angry, take a deep breath and then ask
yourself a simple question: "How would Jesus
behave if He were here?" The answer to that
question will tell you what to do.

Jesus was quick to speak kind words, and
He was quick to forgive others. We must do
our best to be like Him. When we do, we will be
patient, loving, understanding, and kind.

A Thought for Today

We have in Jesus Christ a perfect example of
how to put God's truth into practice.

Bill Bright

It Pays to Praise

Is anyone happy? Let him sing songs of praise.

James 5:13 NIV

The Bible makes it clear: it pays to say "thank You" to God. But sometimes, we may not feel like thanking anybody, not even our Father in heaven.

If we ever stop praising God, it's a big mistake . . . a VERY BIG mistake.

When you stop to think about it, God has been very generous with you . . . and He deserves a great big "thanks" for all those amazing gifts.

Do you want an attitude that pleases God? Then make sure that your attitude praises God. And don't just praise Him on Sunday morning. Praise Him every day, starting with this one.

A Thought for Today

God is worthy of our praise and is pleased when we come before Him with thanksgiving.

Shirley Dobson

Today, Try to Memorize This Verse

Peace I leave with you.
My peace I give to you.
I do not give to you
as the world gives.
Your heart must not be
troubled or fearful.
John 14:27 HCSB

Here's a Bible verse that you should learn.
Practice saying it several times.
And then, talk to mom or dad
about exactly what the verse means.

Keep Learning About Self-Control

Do you not know that the runners in a stadium
all race, but only one receives the prize?
Run in such a way that you may win. Now
everyone who competes exercises self-control
in everything. However, they do it to receive
a perishable crown, but we an imperishable one.

1 Corinthians 9:24-25 HCSB

Who needs to learn more about self-control?
You do! Why? Well, for one thing, you'll discover
that good things happen to people (like you)
who are wise enough to think ahead and smart
enough to look before they leap.

Whether you're at home or at school, you'll
learn that the best rewards go to the kids who
control their behavior—not to the people who
let their behaviors control them!

A Thought for Today

Problems arise if we want the rewards of
success without paying the price.

John Maxwell

Think Ahead

Learn the truth and never reject it.
Get wisdom, self-control, and understanding.
Proverbs 23:23 NCV

Maybe you've heard this old saying: "Look before you leap." What does that saying mean? It means that you should stop and think before you do something. Otherwise, you might be sorry you did it.

Your parents are trying to teach you how to slow down and make better decisions. Why? Because your parents want what's best for you, that's why!

So here's something that you can do: think about the consequences of your behaviors before you do something silly . . . or dangerous . . . or both.

Today's Tip

When you learn how to control yourself, you'll be happier . . . and your parents will be happier, too.

Start Sharing Now

Never walk away from someone who deserves
help; your hand is God's hand for that person.
Proverbs 3:27 MSG

When is the best time to share? Whenever
you can—and that means right now, if possible.
When you start thinking about the things you
can share, you probably think mostly about
things that belong to you (like toys or clothes),
but there are many more things you can share
(like love, kindness, encouragement, and
prayers). That means you have the opportunity
to share something with somebody almost any
time you want. And that's exactly what God
wants you to do—so start sharing now and
don't ever stop.

A Thought for Today

It is the duty of every Christian
to be Christ to his neighbor.
Martin Luther

Big Ideas About...

Perfectionism

Here are two important ideas.
Take a few minutes to talk to your mom or dad
about what these quotations mean.

What makes a Christian a Christian is not perfection but forgiveness.

Max Lucado

The happiest people in the world are not
those who have no problems, but the people
who have learned to live with those things
that are less than perfect.

James Dobson

Counting Your Blessings

Enter his gates with thanksgiving; go into his courts with praise. Give thanks to him and bless his name. For the Lord is good. His unfailing love continues forever, and his faithfulness continues to each generation.

Psalm 100:4-5 NLT

If you sat down and began counting your blessings, how long would it take? A very, very long time! Your blessings include your life, your family, your friends, your talents, and possessions, for starters. But, your greatest blessing—a gift that is yours for the asking—is God's gift of eternal life through Christ Jesus.

You can never count up every single blessing that God has given you, but it doesn't hurt to try . . . so get ready, get set, go—start counting your blessings RIGHT NOW!

Today's Tip

There is value in thanking God for His perfect plan even when you don't understand that plan.

Stop and Think

But now you must also put away all
the following: anger, wrath, malice, slander,
and filthy language from your mouth.

Colossians 3:8 HCSB

When we lose control of our emotions, we do things that we shouldn't do. Sometimes, we throw tantrums. How silly! Other times we pout or whine. Too bad!

The Bible tells us that it is foolish to become angry and that it is wise to remain calm. That's why we should learn to slow down and think about things before we do them.

Do you want to make life better for yourself and for your family? Then be patient and think things through. Stop and think before you do things, not after. It's the wise thing to do.

Today's Tip

If you're a little angry, think carefully before you speak. If you're very angry, think very carefully. Otherwise, you might say something in anger that you regret later.

God's Book

Man shall not live by bread alone,
but by every word that proceeds
from the mouth of God.

Matthew 4:4 NKJV

If you want to know God, you should read
the book He wrote. It's called the Bible (of
course!), and God uses it to teach you and
guide you. The Bible is not like any other book.
It is an amazing gift from your Heavenly Father.

D. L. Moody observed, "The Bible was not
given to increase our knowledge but to change
our lives." God's Holy Word is, indeed, a life-
changing, one-of-a-kind treasure. Handle it with
care, but more importantly, handle it every day!

Today's Tip

Start learning about Jesus, and keep learning
about Him as long as you live. His story never
grows old, and His teachings never fail.

Big Ideas About . . .

Not Giving Up

Here are two important ideas.
Take a few minutes to talk to your mom or dad
about what these quotations mean.

By perseverance the snail
reached the ark.

C. H. Spurgeon

God never gives up on you,
so don't you ever give up
on Him.

Marie T. Freeman

Obedience Is a Choice

Those who obey his commands live in him, and he in them. And this is how we know that he lives in us: We know it by the Spirit he gave us.

1 John 3:24 NIV

You have a choice to make: are you going to be an obedient person or not? And remember: the decision to be obedient—or the decision not to be obedient—is a decision that you must make for yourself.

If you decide to behave yourself you've made a smart choice. If you decide to obey your parents, you've made another smart choice. If you decide to pay attention to your teachers, you've made yet another wise choice. BUT . . . if you decide not to be obedient, you've made a silly choice.

What kind of person will you choose to be? An obedient, well-behaved person . . . or the opposite? Before you answer that question, here's something to think about: obedience pays . . . and disobedience doesn't.

Get Over It

The Lord says, "Forget what happened before,
and do not think about the past.
Look at the new thing I am going to do.
It is already happening. Don't you see it?
I will make a road in the desert
and rivers in the dry land."

Isaiah 43:18-19 NCV

An important part of learning how to forgive is learning how to get over the things that happened yesterday. What happened yesterday is past. And, if what happened yesterday has made you unhappy, today is as good a day as any to start getting over your hurt feelings.

Are you still angry with someone? Has that person said he or she was sorry and tried to make things better? If so, talk to your parents about it! They'll help you understand that you can't change the past, but you can get over it.

Jesus Offers Peace

I have told you these things,
so that in me you may have peace.
In this world you will have trouble.
But take heart! I have overcome the world.
John 16:33 NIV

Jesus offers us peace . . . peace in our hearts and peace in our homes. But He doesn't force us to enjoy His peace—we can either accept His peace or not.

When we accept the peace of Jesus Christ by opening up our hearts to Him, we feel much better about ourselves, our families, and our lives.

Would you like to feel a little better about yourself and a little better about your corner of the world? Then open up your heart to Jesus, because that's where real peace begins.

Today's Tip

You have a big role to play in helping to maintain a peaceful home. It's a big job, so don't be afraid to ask for help . . . especially God's help.

Nobody's Perfect

But God's mercy is great, a
nd he loved us very much.
Ephesians 2:4NCV

Face facts: nobody's perfect . . . not even you! And remember this: it's perfectly okay not to be perfect. In fact, God doesn't expect you to be perfect, and you shouldn't expect yourself to be perfect, either.

Are you one of those people who can't stand to make a mistake? Do you think that you must please everybody all the time? When you make a mess of things, do you become terribly upset? If so, here's some advice: DON'T BE SO HARD ON YOURSELF! Mistakes happen . . . and besides, if you learn something from your mistakes, you'll become a better person.

Today's Tip

The world isn't perfect; your family and friends aren't perfect; and you aren't perfect—and that's okay: We'll all have plenty of time to be perfect in heaven. Until then, we should all be compassionate, forgiving Christians.

What's Really Important

A pretentious, showy life is an empty life;
a plain and simple life is a full life.
Proverbs 13:7 MSG

"So much stuff to shop for, and so little time . . ." These words describe lots of people, but please don't let those words describe you!

The Bible teaches this important lesson: it's not good to be too concerned about money or the stuff that money can buy. So don't worry too much about the things you can buy in stores. Worry more about obeying your parents and obeying your Heavenly Father—that's what's really important.

Today's Tip

Stuff 101: The world says, "Buy more stuff." God says, "Stuff isn't important." Believe God.

Today, Try to Memorize This Verse

Cast your burden on the Lord,
and He will support you;
He will never allow
the righteous to be shaken.

Psalm 55:22 HCSB

Here's a Bible verse that you should learn.
Practice saying it several times.
And then, talk to mom or dad
about exactly what the verse means.

Be Responsible

So then each of us shall give account
of himself to God.

Romans 14:12 NKJV

Nobody can be patient for you. You've got to be patient for yourself. Certainly your parents can teach you about patience, but when it comes to controlling your temper, nobody can control it for you; you've got to control it yourself.

In the Book of Galatians, Paul writes, "We must not tire of doing good." And that's an important lesson: even when we're tired or frustrated, we must do our best to do the right thing.

So the next time you're tempted to lose your temper, stop for a moment and remember that when it comes to good deeds and good behavior, it's all up to you.

You're So Special

Your beliefs about these things should be
kept secret between you and God.
People are happy if they can do what they think
is right without feeling guilty.

Romans 14:22 NCV

When God made you, He made you in a very
special way. In fact, you're a wonderful, one-
of-a-kind creation, a special person unlike any
other.

Do you realize how special you are? Do you
know that God loves you because of who you
are (not because of the things you've done)?
And do you know that God has important
things for you to do? Well, whether you realize
it or not, all these things are all true.

So the next time you feel bad about
something you've done, take a look in the
mirror, and remember that you're looking at a
wonderfully special person . . . you!

God loves you; your parents love you; your
family loves you . . . and that's the way that you
should feel about yourself, too.

Do the Right Thing: Share!

The righteous give without sparing.

Proverbs 21:26 NIV

It's a fact: sharing makes you a better person. Why? Because when you share, you're doing several things: first, you're obeying God; and, you're making your corner of the world a better place; and you're learning exactly what it feels like to be a generous, loving person.

When you share, you have the fun of knowing that your good deeds are making other people happy. When you share, you're learning how to become a better person. When you share, you're making things better for other people and for yourself. So do the right thing: share!

A Thought for Today

Find out how much God has given you
and from it take what you need;
the remainder is needed by others.

St. Augustine

Keep Growing Up

For this reason also, since the day we heard this, we haven't stopped praying for you. We are asking that you may be filled with the knowledge of His will in all wisdom and spiritual understanding.

Colossians 1:9 HCSB

When will you be completely grown up? Hopefully never! God has a way of helping you continue to grow as a Christian throughout your entire life if you continue to worship Him.

If you learn about God's Word and talk to Him through your prayers, He has much to teach you. So keep learning about your Heavenly Father. And never stop.

Today's Tip

Regular, consistent study of God's Word will help ensure that you will continue to grow as a Christian.

A Thankful Attitude?

O come, let us sing unto the LORD:
let us make a joyful noise to the rock
of our salvation. Let us come before
his presence with thanksgiving,
and make a joyful noise unto him with psalms.

Psalm 95:1-2 KJV

Do you have a thankful attitude? Hopefully so! After all, you've got plenty of things to be thankful for. Even during those times when you're angry or tired, you're a very lucky person.

Who has given you all the blessings you enjoy? Your parents are responsible, of course. But all of your blessings really start with God. That's why you should say "Thank You" to God many times each day. He's given you so much . . . so thank Him, starting now.

Today's Tip

Want to cheer yourself up? Count your blessings. If you need a little cheering up, start counting your blessings . . . and keep counting until you feel better.

Waiting Your Turn

Don't be impatient for the Lord to act! Travel steadily along his path. He will honor you....

Psalm 37:34 NLT

When we're standing in line or waiting our turn, it's tempting to scream, "Me first!" It's tempting, but it's the wrong thing to do! The Bible tells us that we shouldn't push ahead of other people; instead, we should do the right thing—and the polite thing—by saying, "You first!"

Sometimes, waiting your turn can be hard, especially if you're excited or in a hurry. But even then, waiting patiently is the right thing to do. Why? Because parents say so, teachers say so, and, most importantly, God says so!

A Thought for Today

It's not difficult to make an impact on your world. All you really have to do is put the needs of others ahead of your own. You can make a difference with a little time and a big heart.

James Dobson

Love Yourself, Too!

God began doing a good work in you,
and I am sure he will continue it until it is
finished when Jesus Christ comes again.
Philippians 1:6 NCV

The Bible teaches you this lesson: you should love everybody—and the word "everybody" includes yourself. Do you treat yourself with honor and respect? You should. After all, God created you in a very special way, and He loves you very much. And if God thinks you are amazing and wonderful, shouldn't you think about yourself in the same way? Of course you should!

So remember this: God wants you to love everybody, including the person you see when you look in the mirror. And one more thing: when you learn how to respect the person in the mirror, you'll be better at respecting other people, too.

Learning How to Share

It is well with the man who deals
generously and lends.

Psalm 112:5 RSV

If you're having a little trouble learning how
to share your stuff, you're not alone! Most
people have problems letting go of things, so
don't be discouraged. Just remember that
learning to share requires practice and lots of
it. The more you share—and the more you learn
how good it feels to share—the sooner you'll be
able to please God with the generosity and love
that flows from your heart.

A Thought for Today

The mind grows by taking in, but the heart
grows by giving out.

Warren Wiersbe

Big Ideas About . . .

Respecting Other People

Here are two important ideas.
Take a few minutes to talk to your mom or dad
about what these quotations mean.

If you are willing to honor a
person out of respect for God,
you can be assured that
God will honor you.

Beth Moore

Don't be a half-Christian.
There are too many of them in the world
already. The world has a profound respect for
a person who is sincere in his faith.

Billy Graham

Be Generous!

And God will generously provide all you need.
Then you will always have everything you need
and plenty left over to share with others.

2 Corinthians 9:8 NLT

The Bible teaches that it's better to be
generous than selfish. But sometimes, you
won't feel like sharing your things, and you'll be
tempted to keep everything for yourself. When
you're feeling a little bit stingy, remember this:
God wants you to share your things, and He will
reward you when you do so.

When you learn to be a more generous
person, God will be pleased with you . . . and
you'll be pleased with yourself. So do yourself
(and everybody else) a favor: be a little more
generous, starting NOW!

Today's Tip

When you are generous with others, God
blesses you even more.

The Blame Game

People's own foolishness ruins their lives,
but in their minds they blame the Lord.
Proverbs 19:3 NCV

When something goes wrong, do you look for somebody to blame? And do you try to blame other people even if you're the one who made the mistake? Hopefully not!

It's silly to try to blame other people for your own mistakes, so don't do it.

If you've done something you're ashamed of, don't look for somebody to blame; look for a way to say, "I'm sorry, and I won't make that same mistake again."

Today's Tip

It's very tempting to blame others when you make a mistake, but it's more honest to look in the mirror first.

Give Your Full Attention

Let the wise listen and add to their learning,
and let the discerning get guidance.

Proverbs 1:5 NIV

Have you learned how to sit quietly and listen to your parents and your teachers? Have you learned how to listen respectfully—with your ears open wide and your mouth closed tight? If so, give yourself a big pat on the back (or if you can't reach way back there, ask your mom or dad to do it for you!)

An important part of learning self-control is learning how to be quiet when you're supposed to be quiet. It isn't always easy, but the sooner you learn how to sit quietly and behave respectfully, the better. So you might as well start today.

Today's Tip

Listen first, then speak: For most people, the temptation to talk is great; it takes conscious effort to hold one's tongue until one's ears are fully engaged. When a person is able to do so, his or her efforts are usually rewarded.

Peace at Home

My dear brothers, always be willing to listen
and slow to speak. Do not become angry easily.
Anger will not help you live
a good life as God wants.

James 1:19 ICB

Sometimes, it's easy to become angry with
the people we love most, and sometimes it's
hard to forgive them. After all, we know that
our family will still love us no matter how angry
we become. But while it's easy to become angry
at home, it's usually wrong.

The next time you're tempted to stay angry
at a brother, or a sister, or a parent, remember
that these are the people who love you more
than anybody else! Then, calm down, and
forgive them . . . NOW! Because peace is always
beautiful, especially when it's peace at your
house.

A Thought for Today

When you strike out in anger, you may miss the
other person, but you will always hit yourself.

Jim Gallery

Today, Try to Memorize This Verse

Let us not become weary
in doing good,
for at the proper time
we will reap a harvest
if we do not give up.
Galatians 6:9 NIV

Here's a Bible verse that you should learn.
Practice saying it several times.
And then, talk to mom or dad
about exactly what the verse means.

What Your Conscience Says About Forgiveness

Now the goal of our instruction is love from a pure heart, a good conscience, and a sincere faith.

1 Timothy 1:5 HCSB

God gave you something called a conscience: it's that little feeling that tells you whether something is right or wrong. Your conscience will usually tell you what to do and when to do it. Trust that feeling.

If you listen to your conscience, it won't be as hard for you to forgive people. Why? Because forgiving other people is the right thing to do. And, it's what God wants you to do. And it's what your conscience tells you to do. So what are you waiting for?

Today's Tip

Trust the quiet inner voice of your conscience: Treat your conscience as you would a trusted advisor.

When People Are Cruel

A kind person is doing himself a favor.
But a cruel person brings trouble upon himself.
Proverbs 11:17 ICB

Face it: sometimes people can be cruel.
And when people are unkind to you or to your
friends, you may be tempted to strike back in
anger. Don't do it! Instead, remember that God
corrects other people's behaviors in His own
way, and He doesn't need your help. So even
when other people misbehave, God wants you
to forgive them . . . and that's what you should
do.

A Thought for Today

A keen sense of humor helps us to overlook the
unbecoming, understand the unconventional,
tolerate the unpleasant, overcome the
unexpected, and outlast the unbearable.
Billy Graham

His Joy, Your Joy

I've told you these things for a purpose:
that my joy might be your joy,
and your joy wholly mature.

John 15:11 MSG

Christ made it clear to His followers: He intended that His joy would become their joy. And it still holds true today: Christ intends that His believers share His love with His joy in their hearts. Yet sometimes, amid the inevitable hustle and bustle of life-here-on-earth, we can forfeit—albeit temporarily—the joy of Christ as we wrestle with the challenges of daily living.

C. H. Spurgeon, the 19th century English clergyman, advised, "The Lord is glad to open the gate to every knocking soul. It opens very freely. Have faith and enter at this moment through holy courage. If you knock with a heavy heart, you shall yet sing with joy of spirit. Never be discouraged!" How true!

How Do They Know?

Do you want to be counted wise, to build
a reputation for wisdom? Here's what you do:
Live well, live wisely, live humbly.
It's the way you live, not the way you talk,
that counts.

James 3:13 MSG

How do people know that you're a
Christian? Well, you can tell them, of course.
And make no mistake about it: talking about
your faith in God is a very good thing to
do. But simply telling people about Jesus
isn't enough. You must also be willing to
show people how a real Christian (like you)
should behave. Does that sound like a big
responsibility? It is . . . but you can do it!

Today's Tip

The life you live is your most important
testimony.

Willing To Forgive

Get along with each other, and forgive each other. If someone does wrong to you, forgive that person because the Lord forgave you.

Colossians 3:13 NCV

The Bible tells us this: When other people do things that are wrong, we should forgive them. God's Word also tells us that when we're willing to forgive others, God is quick to forgive us for the mistakes that we make.

Has somebody done something that makes you angry? Talk things over with your mom or dad, and then be ready to forgive the person who has hurt your feelings. And remember: God wants you to hurry up and forgive others, just like God is always in a hurry to forgive you.

Today's Tip

If forgiveness were easy, everybody would be doing it—but it's not always easy to forgive and forget. If you simply can't seem to forgive somebody, pray about it . . . and keep praying about it . . . until God helps you do the right thing.

Positive Peer Pressure

My dear, dear friends, if God loved us like this,
we certainly ought to love each other.
1 John 4:11 MSG

Are your friends the kind of kids who
encourage you to behave yourself? If so, you've
chosen your friends wisely.

But if your friends try to get you in trouble,
perhaps it's time to think long and hard about
making some new friends.

Whether you know it or not, you're probably
going to behave like your friends behave. So
pick out friends who make you want to behave
better, not worse. When you do, you'll be saving
yourself from a lot of trouble . . . a whole lot of
trouble.

Today's Tip

Choose wise friends, and listen carefully to the
advice that they give.

Big Ideas About . . .

Faith

Here are two important ideas.
Take a few minutes to talk to your mom or dad
about what these quotations mean.

Faith is seeing light with the eyes
of your heart, when the eyes of
your body see only darkness.

Barbara Johnson

It's not the strength of your faith that's
important. It's the object of your faith.
If you are trusting God, then you will receive
all that God can give you.

Warren Wiersbe

God Cares About You!

For He is gracious and compassionate,
slow to anger, rich in faithful love.
Joel 2:13 HCSB

If God had a refrigerator in heaven, your picture would be on it! And that fact should make you feel very good about the person you are and the person you can become.

God's love for you is bigger and more wonderful than you can imagine, So do this, and do it right now: accept God's love with open arms and welcome His Son Jesus into your heart. When you do, you'll feel better about yourself . . . and your life will be changed forever.

Today's Tip

Remember: God's love for you is too big to understand with your brain . . . but it's not too big to feel with your heart.

He Is Everywhere

God did this so that men would seek him and
perhaps reach out for him and find him,
though he is not far from each one of us.
Acts 17:27 NIV

God is everywhere you have ever been. And
He is everywhere you will ever go. That's why
you can speak to God any time you need to.

If you are afraid or discouraged, you can
turn to God for strength. If you are worried,
you can trust God's promises. And if you are
happy, you can thank Him for His gifts.

God is right here, and so are you. And He's
waiting patiently to hear from you, so why not
have a word with Him right now?

Today's Tip

Seek God's presence and wisdom allowing Him
to influence your decisions throughout the day.

The Good In Others, And You

The Lord is gracious and compassionate,
slow to anger and great in faithful love.
The Lord is good to everyone; His compassion
[rests] on all He has made.

Psalm 145:8-9 HCSB

If you look for the good in other people,
you'll probably find it. And, if you look for the
good things in life, you'll probably find them,
too.

But if you spend your time looking for
things that aren't so good, you'll most certainly
find plenty of bad things to look at. So what
should you do? It's simple: you should look for
the good things, of course.

When you start looking for good things,
you'll find them everywhere: in church, at
school, in your neighborhood, and at home.

So don't waste your time on things that
make you feel angry, discouraged, worried,
guilty, or afraid. Look, instead, for the good
things in life, the things that God wants you to
pay attention to. You'll be glad you did . . . and
God will be glad, too.

Each Day Is a Gift

How happy are those who can live in your house, always singing your praises. How happy are those who are strong in the Lord....

Psalm 84:4-5 NLT

God wants you to have a happy, joyful life. But that doesn't mean that you'll be happy all the time. Sometimes, you won't feel like feeling happy, and when you don't, your attitude won't be very good.

When you're feeling a little tired or sad, here's something to remember: This day is a gift from God. And it's up to you to enjoy this day by trying to be cheerful, helpful, courteous, and well-behaved. How can you do these things? A good place to start is by doing your best to think good thoughts.

Today's Tip

To make happiness last, we must obey God while celebrating His blessings. To make happiness disappear, we need only disobey God while ignoring His blessings.

A Royal Law

This royal law is found in the Scriptures:
"Love your neighbor as yourself."
If you obey this law, then you are doing right.

James 2:8 ICB

James was the brother of Jesus and a leader of the early Christian church. In a letter that is now a part of the New Testament, James reminded his friends of a "royal law." That law is the Golden Rule.

When we treat others in the same way that we wish to be treated, we are doing the right thing. James knew it and so, of course did his brother, Jesus. Now we should learn the same lesson: it's nice to be nice; it's good to be good; and it's great to be kind.

A Thought for Today

Encouraging others means helping people, looking for the best in them, and trying to bring out their positive qualities.

John Maxwell

Loving People Who Are Hard to Love

Real wisdom, God's wisdom, begins with
a holy life and is characterized by getting
along with others. It is gentle and reasonable,
overflowing with mercy and blessings,
not hot one day and cold the next,
not two-faced.

James 3:17 MSG

Sometimes, people can be rude . . . very
rude. As long as you live here on earth, you
will face countless opportunities to lose your
temper when other folks behave badly. But
God has a better plan: He wants you to forgive
people and move on. Remember that God has
already forgiven you, so it's only right that you
should be willing to forgive others.

So here's some good advice: Forgive
everybody as quickly as you can, and leave the
rest up to God.

Big Ideas About . . .

Hope

Here are two important ideas.
Take a few minutes to talk to your mom or dad
about what these quotations mean.

You can look forward with hope,
because one day there will be
no more separation, no more scars,
and no more suffering in My Father's House.
It's the home of your dreams!

Anne Graham Lotz

And because we know Christ
is alive, we have hope for
the present and hope
for life beyond the grave.

Billy Graham

Always Be Truthful

...and put on the new self, which in the likeness
of God has been created in righteousness and
holiness of the truth. Therefore, laying aside
falsehood, speak truth, each one of you,
with his neighbor, for we are members
of one another.

Ephesians 4:24-25 NASB

If you're tempted to say something that isn't
true, stop and ask yourself a simple question:
"How would Jesus behave if He were here?"
The answer to that question will tell you what
to say.

Jesus told His followers that the truth
would make them free. As believers, we must
do our best to know the truth and to tell it.
When we do, we behave as our Savior behaved,
and that's exactly how God wants us to behave.

Today's Tip

When in doubt: do the thing that you think
Jesus would do. And, of course, don't do
something if you think that He wouldn't do it.

Time With God

Careful planning puts you ahead in the long run; hurry and scurry puts you further behind.
Proverbs 21:5 MSG

How much time do you spend getting to know God? A lot? A little? Almost none? Hopefully, you answered, "a lot."

God loved this world so much that He sent His Son to save it. And now only one real question remains for you: what will you do in response to God's love? God deserves your prayers, your obedience, and your love—and He deserves these things all day every day, not just on Sunday mornings.

Today's Tip

You should plan to spend some time with God every day . . . and you should stick to your plan!

God Is Watching

We must be sure to obey the truth
we have learned already.

Philippians 3:16 NLT

Even when nobody's watching, God is. And
He knows whether you've done the right thing
or the wrong thing. So if you're tempted to
misbehave when nobody is looking, remember
this: There is never a time when "nobody's
watching." Somebody is always watching over
you—and that Somebody, of course, is your
Father in Heaven. Don't let Him down!

Today's Tip

When it comes to telling the world about your
relationship with God . . . your actions speak
much more loudly than your words . . . so
behave accordingly.

The Right Choice

For God has not given us a spirit of fearfulness,
but one of power, love, and sound judgment.

2 Timothy 1:7 HCSB

Your life is a series of choices. From the instant you wake up in the morning until the moment you nod off to sleep at night, you make lots of decisions: decisions about the things you do, decisions about the words you speak, and decisions about the thoughts you choose to think.

So, if you want to lead a life that is pleasing to God, you must make choices that are pleasing to Him. And you know what? He deserves no less . . . and neither, for that matter, do you.

Today's Tip

When you make wise choices, you make everybody happy. You make your parents happy, you make your teachers happy, you make your friends happy, and you make God happy!

Today, Try to Memorize This Verse

For this is the love of God,
that we keep
His commandments.

1 John 5:3 NKJV

Here's a Bible verse that you should learn.
Practice saying it several times.
And then, talk to mom or dad
about exactly what the verse means.

Obey God by Doing the Right thing

Friend, don't go along with evil. Model the good. The person who does good does God's work. The person who does evil falsifies God, doesn't know the first thing about God.

3 John 1:11 MSG

When other people are unkind, you may be tempted to strike back in anger. But God doesn't want you to fight your way through life! God wants you to forgive other people, even when they haven't behaved themselves, even when they've been very mean. So, when other people aren't nice, forgive them as quickly as you can. And let God take care of everything else.

A Thought for Today

God shapes the world by prayer. The more praying there is in the world, the better the world will be, and the mightier will be the forces against evil.

E. M. Bounds

Being a Good Example to Your Friends

We have around us many people whose lives
tell us what faith means. So let us run the race
that is before us and never give up.
We should remove from our lives anything that
would get in the way and the sin that
so easily holds us back.

Hebrews 12:1 NCV

Are you a person whose behavior serves
as a good example for other kids? If so,
congratulations! God smiles upon people (like
you) who do what's right, but that's not all.
God also rewards good behavior when He sees
it (and you can be sure that He sees it!)

So do yourself and your friends a favor: Do
the right thing every chance you get.

Today's Tip

As an example for living, look to Jesus.

Forgive And Forget

And forgive us our sins, for we ourselves
also forgive everyone in debt to us.

Luke 11:4 HCSB

Have you heard the saying, "Forgive and forget?" Well, it's certainly easier said than done. It's easy to talk about forgiving somebody, but actually forgiving that person can be much harder to do. And when it comes to forgetting, forget about it!

Sometimes, it's impossible to forget the people who hurt our feelings. But even if we can't forget, we can forgive. And that's exactly what God teaches us to do.

Today's Tip

Forgive . . . and keep forgiving! Sometimes, you may forgive someone once and then, at a later time, become angry at the very same person again. If so, you must forgive that person again and again . . . until it sticks!

Good Friends Behave

As iron sharpens iron,
so people can improve each other.
Proverbs 27:17 NCV

Our world is filled with pressures: some good, some bad. The pressures that we feel to follow God's rules are the good kind of pressures (and the friends who make us want to obey God are good friends). But sometimes, we may feel pressure to misbehave, pressure from friends who want us to disobey the rules.

If you want to please God and your parents, make friends with people who behave themselves. When you do, you'll be much more likely to behave yourself, too . . . and that's a very good thing.

Today's Tip

If you choose friends who behave themselves . . . you'll be far more likely to behave yourself, too.

Make Them Proud

Give generously,
for your gifts will return to you later.
Ecclesiastes 11:1 NLT

It's tempting to be selfish, but it's wrong. It's tempting to want to keep everything for yourself, but it's better to share. It's tempting to say, "No, that's MINE!" but it's better to say, "I'll share it with you."

Are you sometimes tempted to be a little stingy? Are you sometimes tempted to say, "No, I don't' want to share that!"—and then do you feel a little sorry that you said it? If that describes you, don't worry: everybody is tempted to be a little bit selfish. Your job is to remember this: even when it's tempting to be selfish, you should try very hard not to be. Because when you're generous, not selfish, you'll make your parents proud and you'll make your Father in Heaven proud, too.

Big Ideas About . . .

God's Protection

Here are two important ideas.
Take a few minutes to talk to your mom or dad
about what these quotations mean.

Under heaven's lock and
key, we are protected by the
most efficient security system
available: the power of God.

Charles Swindoll

If the Father knows when a sparrow falls,
don't you think He's aware of where you are,
what your need is, and what your concern is?
Rest in that.

Jack Hayford

God Is With You

Do not fear, for I am with you; do not be afraid, for I am your God. I will strengthen you; I will help you; I will hold on to you with My righteous right hand.

Isaiah 41:10 HCSB

Here's a promise you can depend on: wherever you are, God is always there, too.

God doesn't take vacations, and He doesn't play hide-and-seek. He's always "right here, right now," waiting to hear from you. So if you're wondering where God is, wonder no more. He's here. And that's a promise!

Today's Tip

God's presence provides comfort...seek Him often.

Making Other People (and Yourself) Happy

Anxiety in a man's heart weighs it down,
but a good word cheers it up.

Proverbs 12:25 HCSB

The Bible teaches us to treat other people with respect, kindness, courtesy, and love. When we do, we make other people happy, we make God happy, and we feel better about ourselves, too.

So, if you're wondering how to make the world—and your world—a better place, here's a great place to start: let the Golden Rule be your rule. When you do, you'll like yourself a little better . . . and so will other people.

Today's Tip

When you treat others with respect, you will feel better about yourself.

Today's Happiness

But happy are those . . .
whose hope is in the LORD their God.
Psalm 146:5 NLT

If we could decide to be happy "once and for all," life would be so much simpler, but it doesn't seem to work that way. If we want happiness to last, we need to create good thoughts every day that we live. Yesterday's good thoughts don't count . . . we've got to think more good thoughts today.

Each new day is a gift from God, so treat it that way. Think about it like this: today is another wonderful chance to celebrate God's gifts.

So celebrate—starting now—and keep celebrating forever!

Today's Tip

Better self-control can help make you happy: the better you behave, the more fun you'll have. And don't let anybody try to tell you otherwise.

An Honest Heart

Lying lips are detestable to the Lord.
Proverbs 12:22 HCSB

Where does honesty begin? It begins in your own heart and your own head. If you sincerely want to be an honest person, then you must ask God to help you find the courage and the determination to be honest all of the time.

Honesty is not a "sometimes" thing. If you intend to be a truthful person, you must make truthfulness a habit that becomes so much a part of you that you don't have to decide whether or not you're going to tell the truth. Instead, you will simply tell the truth because it's the kind of person you are.

Lying is an easy habit to fall into, and a terrible one. So, make up your mind that you're going to be an honest person, and then stick to your decision. That's what your parents want you to do, and that's what God wants, too. And since they love you more than you know, trust them. And always tell the truth.

God's Friendship

Greater love has no one than this,
that he lay down his life for his friends.
John 15:13 NIV

There's an old song that says, "What a friend we have in Jesus." Those words are certainly true! When you invite Him into your heart, Jesus will be your friend forever. If you make mistakes, He'll still be your friend. If you behave badly, He'll still love you. If you feel sorry or sad, He can help you feel better if you ask Him to.

Jesus wants you to have a happy, healthy life. He wants you to behave yourself, and He wants you to take care of yourself. And now, it's up to you to do your best to live up to the hopes and dreams of your very best friend: Jesus.

A Thought for Today

God soon turns from his wrath,
but he never turns from his love.
C. H. Spurgeon

You're Not Expected to Be Perfect

If we confess our sins to him, he is faithful
and just to forgive us and to cleanse us
from every wrong.

1 John 1:9 NLT

When you make a mistake, do you get really
mad at yourself . . . or maybe really, really,
really mad? Hopefully not! After all, everybody
makes mistakes, and nobody is expected to be
perfect.

Even when you make mistakes, God loves
you . . . so you should love yourself, too.

So the next time you make a mistake, learn
from it. And after you've learned your lesson,
try never to make that same mistake again. But
don't be too hard on yourself. God doesn't
expect you to be perfect, and since He loves
you anyway, you should feel that way, too.

Today's Tip

A mistake is never permanent (unless you do
nothing to fix it).

More and More Stuff

Don't be obsessed with getting more
material things. Be relaxed with what you have.
Hebrews 13:5 MSG

Here's something to remember about stuff:
It's not that important!

Lots of people are in love with money and
the things that money can buy. God is not. God
cares about people, not possessions, and so
must you.

You should not be too concerned about
the clothes you wear, or the things you own.
And above all, don't ever let your self-esteem
depend upon the things that you (or your
parents) own.

The stuff that you own isn't nearly as
important as the love that you feel in your
heart—love for your family, love for your
friends, and love for your Father in heaven.

Today's Tip

Your possessions are actually God's possessions,
so try to use them for His purposes.

Big Ideas About . . .

Asking God

Here are two important ideas.
Take a few minutes to talk to your mom or dad
about what these quotations mean.

God uses our most stumbling,
faltering faith-steps as the open
door to His doing for us
"more than we ask or think."
Catherine Marshall

Some people think God does not like to be
troubled with our constant asking.
But, the way to trouble God
is not to come at all.
D. L. Moody

It's Not Hard to Be Kind

Reckless words pierce like a sword,
but the tongue of the wise brings healing.
Proverbs 12:18 NIV

How hard is it to say a kind word? Not very! Yet sometimes we're so busy that we forget to say the very things that might make other people feel better.

We should always try to say nice things to our families and friends. And when we feel like saying something that's not so nice, perhaps we should stop and think before we say it. Kind words help; cruel words hurt. It's as simple as that. And, when we say the right thing at the right time, we give a gift that can change someone's day or someone's life.

Today's Tip

It's good to tell your family how you feel about them, but that's not enough. You should also show them how you feel with your good deeds and your kind words.

Be a Careful Listener

Listen carefully to wisdom;
set your mind on understanding.
Proverbs 2:2 NCV

Do you listen carefully to the things your parents tell you? You should. Your parents want the very best for you. They want you to be happy and healthy; they want you to be smart and to do smart things. Your parents have much to teach you, and you have much to learn. So listen carefully to the things your mom and dad have to say. And ask lots of questions. When you do, you'll soon discover that your parents have lots of answers . . . lots of very good answers.

A Thought for Today

Listening is loving.
Zig Ziglar

God Teaches

I will instruct you and teach you
in the way you should go; I will counsel you
and watch over you.

Psalm 32:8 NIV

The Bible says that when people make mistakes, God corrects them. And that means that if you make a mistake, God will try to find a way to teach you how to keep from making that same mistake again.

God doesn't expect you to be perfect, but He does expect you to learn from your mistakes—NOW!

Today's Tip

When you make a mistake, learn something . . . and forgive someone: yourself. Remember, you don't have to be perfect to be wonderful.

The Best Time to Be Obedient

The one who has My commandments and keeps them is the one who loves Me. And the one who loves Me will be loved by My Father. I also will love him and will reveal Myself to him.

John 14:21 HCSB

If you look in a dictionary, you'll see that the word "wisdom" means "using good judgement, and knowing what is true." But there's more: it's not enough just to know what's right; if you really want to become a wise person, you must also do what's right.

A big part of "doing what's right" is learning to be obedient . . . and the best time to start being a more obedient person is right now! Why? Because it's the wise thing to do.

Today's Tip

Do not willingly put yourself in situations where you might be easily tempted to disobey God.

Patience and the Golden Rule

Be patient when trouble comes.
Pray at all times.
Romans 12:12 ICB

Jesus gave us a Golden Rule for living: He said that we should treat other people in the same way that we want to be treated. And because we want other people to be patient with us, we, in turn, must be patient with them.

Being patient with other people means treating them with kindness, respect, and understanding. It means waiting our turn when we're standing in line and forgiving our friends when they've done something we don't like. Sometimes, it's hard to be patient, but we've got to do our best. And when we do, we're following the Golden Rule—God's rule for how to treat others—and everybody wins!

Today's Tip

Patience is not idlely waiting but it is an activity that means watching and waiting for God to lead you.

When Friends Misbehave

Whoever walks with the wise will become wise; whoever walks with fools will suffer harm.
Proverbs 13:20 NLT

If you're like most people, you have probably been tempted to "go along with the crowd" . . . even when the crowd was misbehaving. But here's something to think about: just because your friends may be misbehaving, doesn't mean that you have to misbehave, too.

When people behave badly, they can spoil things in a hurry. So make sure that they don't spoil things for you.

So, if your friends misbehave, don't copy them! Instead, do the right thing. You'll be glad you did . . . and so will God!

Today's Tip

Remember that it's more important to be respected than to be liked.

Finish What You Start

*We say they are happy because
they did not give up.*

James 5:11 NCV

Jesus finished what He began, and so should you. Jesus didn't give in, and neither should you. Jesus did what was right, and so should you.

Are you facing something that is hard for you to do? If so, you may be tempted to quit. If so, remember this: whatever your problem, God can handle it. Your job is to keep working until He does.

Today's Tip

If things don't work out at first, don't quit. If you never try, you'll never know how good you can be.

Big Ideas About . . .

Your Troubles and Your Prayers

Here are two important ideas.
Take a few minutes to talk to your mom or dad
about what these quotations mean.

When problems threaten to engulf
us, we must do what believers
have always done, turn to the Lord
for encouragement.

Shirley Dobson

The moment anxious thoughts invade
your mind, go to the Lord in prayer.
Look first to God. Then, you will see the cause
of your anxiety in a whole new light.

Kay Arthur

Controling Angry Outbursts

Don't let your spirit rush to be angry,
for anger abides in the heart of fools.
Ecclesiastes 7:9 HCSB

When you're angry, you will be tempted to say things and do things that you'll regret later. So don't do them! Instead of doing things in a hurry, slow down long enough to calm yourself down.

Jesus does not intend that you strike out against other people, and He doesn't intend that your heart be troubled by anger. Your heart should instead be filled with love, just like Jesus' heart was . . . and is!

Today's Tip

You can always say, "Time out!" If you become angry, the best time to step away from the situation is before you say unkind words or do unkind things—not after. It's perfectly okay to place yourself in "time out" until you can calm down.

Self-Control and Patience

All athletes practice strict self-control.
They do it to win a prize that will fade away,
but we do it for an eternal prize.

1 Corinthians 9:25 NLT

The Book of Proverbs tells us that self-control and patience are very good things to have. But for most of us, self-control and patience can also be very hard things to learn.

Are you having trouble being patient? And are you having trouble slowing down long enough to think before you act? If so, remember that self-control takes practice, and lots of it, so keep trying. And if you make a mistake, don't be too upset. After all, if you're going to be a really patient person, you shouldn't just be patient with others; you should also be patient with yourself.

When You Don't Know What to Say

Watch the way you talk. Let nothing foul or
dirty come out of your mouth.
Say only what helps, each word a gift.

Ephesians 4:29 MSG

Sometimes, it's hard to know exactly what
to say. And sometimes, it can be very tempting
to say something that isn't true—or something
that isn't nice. But when you say things you
shouldn't say, you'll regret it later.

So make this promise to yourself, and keep
it—promise to think about the things you say
before you say them. And whatever you do,
always tell the truth. When you do these things,
you'll be doing yourself a big favor, and you'll be
obeying the Word of God.

Today's Tip

Think first, speak second. If you want to keep
from hurting other people's feelings, don't open
your mouth until you've turned on your brain.

Showing People What It Means to Be a Christian

> But respect Christ as the holy Lord
> in your hearts. Always be ready to answer
> everyone who asks you to explain
> about the hope you have.
>
> 1 Peter 3:15 NCV

Every Christian, each in his or her own way, has a responsibility to share the Good News of our Jesus. And it's important to remember that we bear testimony through both words and actions. Wise Christians follow the advice of St. Francis of Assisi who advised, "Preach the gospel at all times and, if necessary, use words."

As you think about how your example influences others, remember that actions speak louder than words . . . much louder!

Today's Tip

You share your testimony through words and actions.

A Pleasing Attitude

Set your minds on what is above,
not on what is on the earth.

Colossians 3:2 HCSB

God knows everything about you, including your attitude. And when your attitude is good, God is pleased . . . very pleased.

Are you interested in pleasing God? Are you interested in pleasing your parents? Your teachers? And your friends? If so, try to make your attitude the best it can be. When you try hard to have a good attitude, you'll make other people feel better—and you'll make yourself feel better, too.

Today's Tip

Remember that you can choose to have a good attitude or a not-so good attitude. And it's a choice you make every day.

When We're Worried

Give all your worries and cares to God,
for he cares about what happens to you.
1 Peter 5:6 NLT

When we're worried, there are two places we should take our concerns: to the people who love and care for us and to God.

When troubles arise, it helps to talk about them with parents, grandparents, and concerned adults. But we shouldn't stop there: we should also talk to God through our prayers.

If you're worried about something, you can pray about it any time you want. And remember that God is always listening, and He always wants to hear from you.

So when you're worried, try this plan: talk and pray. Talk to the grownups who love you, and pray to the Heavenly Father who made you. The more you talk and the more you pray, the better you'll feel.

Don't Whine!

Words kill, words give life;
they're either poison or fruit—you choose.
Proverbs 18:21 MSG

Do you like to listen to other children whine? No way! And since you don't like to hear other kids whining, then you certainly shouldn't whine, either.

Sometimes, kids think that whining is a good way to get the things they want . . . but it's not! So, if your parents or your teacher ask you to do something, don't complain about it. And if there's something you want, don't whine and complain until you get it.

Remember: whining won't make you happy . . . and it won't make anybody else happy, either.

Today's Tip

Whining can be contagious, so make sure that your home is, to the greatest extent possible, a whine-free zone. How can you do this? A good way to start is by counting your blessings, not your problems.

Because You're a Christian

Make the Master proud of you by being good
citizens. Respect the authorities,
whatever their level; they are God's emissaries
for keeping order.

1 Peter 2:13-14 MSG

Do you behave differently because you're
a Christian? Or do you behave in pretty much
the same way that you would if you had never
heard of Jesus? Hopefully, your behavior is
better because of the things you've learned
from the Bible.

Doing the right thing is not always easy,
especially when you're tired or frustrated. But,
doing the wrong thing almost always leads to
trouble. So here's some advice: remember the
lessons you learn from the Bible. And keep
remembering them every day of your life.

Today's Tip

If you're not sure that it's the right thing to do,
don't do it! And if you're not sure that it's the
truth, don't tell it.

Every Day Is a Special Day

Encourage one another daily,
as long as it is Today....
Hebrews 3:13 NIV

Today is a day of celebration, and hopefully, you feel like celebrating! After all, today (like every other day) should be a special time to thank God for all the wonderful things He has given you.

So don't wait for birthdays or holidays— make every day a special day, including this one. Take time to pause and thank God for His gifts. He deserves your thanks, and you deserve to celebrate!

A Thought for Today

If you can forgive the person you were, accept the person you are, and believe in the person you will become, you are headed for joy. So celebrate your life.

Barbara Johnson

That Little Voice

For God is pleased with you when,
for the sake of your conscience,
you patiently endure unfair treatment.
1 Peter 2:19 NLT

When you know that you're doing what's right, you'll feel better about yourself. Why? Because you have a little voice in your head called your "conscience." Your conscience is a feeling that tells you whether something is right or wrong—and it's a feeling that makes you feel better about yourself when you know you've done the right thing.

Your conscience is an important tool. Pay attention to it!

The more you listen to your conscience, the easier it is to behave yourself. So here's great advice: first, slow down long enough to figure out the right thing to do—and then do it! When you do, you'll be proud of yourself . . . and other people will be proud of you, too.

When Things Go Wrong

But as for you, be strong; don't be discouraged,
for your work has a reward.

2 Chronicles 15:7 HCSB

Face facts: some days are more wonderful than other days. Sometimes, everything seems to go right, and on other days, many things seem to go wrong. But here's something to remember: even when you're disappointed with the way things turn out, God is near . . . and He loves you very much!

If you're disappointed, worried, sad, or afraid, you can talk to your parents and to God. And you certainly feel better when you do!

A Thought for Today

Often God has to shut a door in our face so that he can subsequently open the door through which he wants us to go.

Catherine Marshall

Today, Try to Memorize This Verse

I remind you to fan into flame
the gift of God.

2 Timothy 1:6 NIV

Here's a Bible verse that you should learn.
Practice saying it several times.
And then, talk to mom or dad
about exactly what the verse means.

A Cheerful Heart

Jacob said, "For what a relief it is to see your friendly smile. It is like seeing the smile of God!"
Genesis 33:10 NLT

The Bible tells us that a cheerful heart is like medicine: it makes us feel better. Where does cheerfulness begin? It begins inside each of us; it begins in the heart. So let's be thankful to God for His blessings, and let's show our thanks by sharing good cheer wherever we go.

Today, make sure that you share a smile and a kind word with as many people as you can. This old world needs all the cheering up it can get . . . and so do your friends.

Today's Tip

Do you need a little cheering up? If so, find somebody else who needs cheering up, too. Then, do your best to brighten that person's day. When you do, you'll discover that cheering up other people is a wonderful way to cheer yourself up, too!

Encourage Each Other

So encourage each other and give each other
strength, just as you are doing now.
1 Thessalonians 5:11 NCV

When other people are sad, what can we
do? We can do our best to cheer them up by
showing kindness and love.

The Bible tells us that we must care for
each other, and when everybody is happy, that's
an easy thing to do. But, when people are sad,
for whatever reason, it's up to us to speak a
kind word or to offer a helping hand.

Do you know someone who is discouraged
or sad? If so, perhaps it's time to take matters
into your own hands. Think of something you
can do to cheer that person up . . . and then do
it! You'll make two people happy.

Today's Tip

Do you want to be successful and go far in life?
Encourage others to do the same. You can't
lift other people up without lifting yourself up,
too.

Today, Try to Memorize This Verse

I can do all things
through Christ,
because he gives me strength.

Philippians 4:13 NCV

Here's a Bible verse that you should learn.
Practice saying it several times.
And then, talk to mom or dad
about exactly what the verse means.

Daily Devotionals

Stay clear of silly stories that get dressed up
as religion. Exercise daily in God . . . .

1 Timothy 4:7 MSG

Want to know God better? Then schedule a
meeting with Him every day.

Each day has 1,440 minutes—will you spend
a few of those minutes with your Heavenly
Father? He deserves that much of your time
and more. God wants you to pay attention to
Him. So, if you haven't already done so, form
the habit of spending quality time with your
Creator. He deserves it . . . and so, for that
matter, do you.

Today's Tip

Do you have a special place where you and
your parents read daily devotionals? If not, you
should ask your mom or dad to help you think
of a good place where the two of you can read
the Bible and talk to God.

Don't Cry "Wolf!"

I have no greater joy than this: to hear that
my children are walking in the truth.
3 John 1:4 HCSB

Perhaps you've heard the story of the
boy who cried "wolf!" In that story, the boy
exaggerated his problems and eventually got
himself into BIG trouble!

When we pretend that our troubles are
worse than they really are, we may earn a little
sympathy now, but we'll invite lots of trouble
later.

If you're ever tempted to cry "wolf," don't.
Exaggeration wasn't good for the boy who
cried "wolf," and it's not good for you.

Today's Tip

Don't exaggerate! All of us have enough
troubles without pretending that we have
more.

The Powerful Life

God's Way is not a matter of mere talk;
it's an empowered life.

1 Corinthians 4:20 MSG

How do people know that you're a
Christian? Well, you can tell them, of course.
And make no mistake about it: talking about
your faith in God is a very good thing to do.
But telling people about Jesus isn't enough.
You should also show people how a Christian
(like you) should behave.

God wants you to be loving and giving.
That way, when another person sees how you
behave, that person will know what it means to
be a good Christian . . . a good Christian like
you!

A Thought for Today

I have simply tried to do what seemed best
each day, as each day came.

Abraham Lincoln

When You Forgive, You Do Yourself a Big Favor

And whenever you stand praying,
if you have anything against anyone,
forgive him, so that your Father in heaven
may also forgive you your wrongdoing.

Mark 11:25 HCSB

When you forgive somebody else, you're actually doing yourself a favor. Why? Because when you forgive the other person, you get rid of angry feelings that can make you unhappy.

Are you still angry about something that happened yesterday, or the day before that, or the day before that? Do yourself a big favor: forgive everybody (including yourself, if necessary). When you do, you won't change what happened yesterday, but you will make today a whole lot better.

Today's Tip

If you're having trouble forgiving someone else . . . think how many times other people have forgiven you!

Love That Lasts

If I speak the languages of men and of angels,
but do not have love, I am a sounding gong
or a clanging cymbal.

1 Corinthians 13:1 HCSB

Are your friends kind to you? And are
your friends nice to other people, too? If so,
congratulations! If not, it's probably time to
start looking for a few new friends. After
all, it's really not very much fun to be around
people who aren't nice to everybody.

The Bible teaches that a pure heart is a
wonderful blessing. It's up to each of us to fill
our hearts with love for God, love for Jesus,
and love for all people. When we do, we feel
better about ourselves.

Do you want to be the best person you can
be? Then invite the love of Christ into your
heart and share His love with your family and
friends. And remember that lasting love always
comes from a pure heart . . . like yours!

Gentle Words

Always be humble, gentle, and patient,
accepting each other in love.

Ephesians 4:2 NCV

The Bible tells us that gentle words are helpful and that cruel words are not. But sometimes, especially when we're angry or frustrated, our words and our actions may not be so gentle. Sometimes, we may say things or do things that are unkind or hurtful to others. When we do, we're wrong.

So the next time you're tempted to strike out in anger, don't. And if you want to help your family and friends, remember that gentle words are better than harsh words and good deeds are better than the other kind. Always!

A Thought for Today

I choose gentleness. Nothing is won by force.
I choose to be gentle. If I raise my voice may it
be only in praise. If I clench my fist,
may it be only in prayer. If I make a demand,
may it be only of myself.

Max Lucado

God's Promise Of Love

His banner over me was love.
Song of Solomon 2:4 KJV

In the Bible, God makes this amazing promise—He promises that He loves you. And it's a promise He intends to keep.

No matter where you are (and no matter what you've done), you're never beyond the reach of God's love. So take time today (and every day) to thank Him for love that is too big to understand with your head, but not too big to feel with your heart.

A Thought for Today

The life of faith is a daily exploration of the constant and countless ways in which God's grace and love are experienced.
Eugene Peterson

Big Ideas About . . .

Patience

Here are two important ideas.
Take a few minutes to talk to your mom or dad
about what these quotations mean.

In the Bible, patience is not a passive
acceptance of circumstances.
It is a courageous perseverance
in the face of suffering and difficulty.
Warren Wiersbe

We must learn to wait.
There is grace supplied
to the one who waits.
Mrs. Charles E. Cowman

Obey God, Be Happy

I will praise you, Lord, with all my heart.
I will tell all the miracles you have done.
I will be happy because of you; God Most High,
I will sing praises to your name.

Psalm 9:1-2 NCV

Do you want to be happy? Here are some things you should do: Love God and His Son, Jesus; obey the Golden Rule; and always try to do the right thing. When you do these things, you'll discover that happiness goes hand-in-hand with good behavior.

The happiest people do not misbehave; the happiest people are not cruel or greedy. They don't say unkind things. The happiest people are those who love God and follow His rules— starting, of course, with the Golden one.

Today's Tip

Remember: through good times and bad, you'll always be happier if you obey the rules of your Father in heaven. So obey them!

God Knows Your Heart

Create in me a pure heart, God,
and make my spirit right again.
Psalm 51:10 NCV

Other people see you from the outside. God sees you from the inside—God sees your heart.

Kindness comes from the heart. So does sharing. So if you want to show your family and your friends that your heart is filled with kindness and love, one way to do it is by sharing. But don't worry about trying to show God what kind of person you are. He already knows your heart, and He loves you more than you can imagine.

A Thought for Today

The God who dwells in heaven is willing to dwell also in the heart of the humble believer.
Warren Wiersbe

Honesty at Home

Good people will be guided by honesty.
Proverbs 11:3 ICB

Should you be honest with your parents? Certainly. With your brothers and sisters? Of course. With cousins, grandparents, aunts and uncles? Yes! In fact, you should be honest with everybody in your family because honesty starts at home.

If you can't be honest in your own house, how can you expect to be honest in other places, like at church or at school? So make sure that you're completely honest with your family. If you are, then you're much more likely to be honest with everybody else.

Today's Tip

If you're tempted to say something that isn't true, don't say anything. A closed mouth tells no lies.

Rejoice!

From the rising of the sun to its setting,
the name of the LORD is to be praised.

Psalm 113:3 NASB

A man named C. S. Lewis once said, "Joy is the serious business of heaven." And he was right! God seriously wants you to be a seriously joyful person.

One way that you can have a more joyful life is by learning how to become a more obedient person. When you do, you'll stay out of trouble, and you'll have lots more time for fun.

So here's a way to be a more joyful, happy person: do the right thing! It's the best way to live.

A Thought for Today

Joy comes not from what we have
but from what we are.

C. H. Spurgeon

Sharing Love and Kindness

Talk and act like a person expecting to be
judged by the Rule that sets us free. For if you
refuse to act kindly, you can hardly expect to
be treated kindly. Kind mercy wins over
harsh judgment every time.

James 2:12-13 MSG

Where does kindness start? It starts in our
hearts and works its way out from there. Jesus
taught us that a pure heart is a wonderful
blessing. It's up to each of us to fill our hearts
with love for God, love for Jesus, and love for
all people. When we do, we are blessed.

Do you want to be the best person you can
be? Then invite the love of Christ into your
heart and share His love with your family and
friends. And remember that lasting love always
comes from a pure heart . . . like yours!

Today's Tip

Everybody is important to God. And you should
treat every person with courtesy, dignity and
respect.

Today, Try to Memorize This Verse

Trust in the LORD
with all your heart;
do not depend on your own
understanding.
Seek his will in all you do,
and he will direct your paths.
Proverbs 3:5-6 NLT

Here's a Bible verse that you should learn.
Practice saying it several times.
And then, talk to mom or dad
about exactly what the verse means.

Living by God's Rules

Therefore, whether we are at home or away, we make it our aim to be pleasing to Him. For we must all appear before the judgment seat of Christ, so that each may be repaid for what he has done in the body, whether good or bad.

2 Corinthians 5:9-10 HCSB

God has rules, and He wants you to obey them. He wants you to be fair, honest, and kind. He wants you to behave yourself, and He wants you to respect your parents. God has other rules, too, and you'll find them in a very special book: the Bible.

With a little help from your parents, you can figure out God's rules. And then, it's up to you to live by them. When you do, everybody will be pleased—you'll be pleased, your parents will be pleased . . . and God will be pleased, too.

Today's Tip

When you obey God, you feel better about yourself.

When Bad Things Happen

I will not leave you comfortless:
I will come to you.
John 14:18 KJV

When bad things happen, it's understandable that we might feel afraid. In fact, it's good to be afraid if our fears keep us from behaving foolishly (by the way, if that little voice inside your head tells you that doing something is dangerous, don't do it).

When our own troubles—or the world's troubles—leave us fearful, we should discuss our concerns with the people who love and care for us. Parents and grandparents can help us understand our fears, and they can help us feel better. That's why we need to talk with them.

It's okay to be afraid—all of us are fearful from time to time. And it's good to know that we can talk about our fears with loved ones and with God. When we do, we'll discover that fear lasts for a little while, but love lasts forever.

Follow Jesus

Follow Me, Jesus told them, "and I will make you into fishers of men!" Immediately they left their nets and followed Him.

Mark 1:17-18 HCSB

Who will you walk with today? Do yourself a favor—walk with Jesus!

God's Word promises that when you follow in Christ's footsteps, you will learn how to behave yourself, and you'll learn how to live a good life. Jesus wants you to be a "new creation" through Him. And that's exactly what you should want for yourself, too. So talk with Jesus (through prayer) and walk with Him (by obeying His rules) today and forever.

Today's Tip

If You Want to be a Disciple of Christ . . . follow in His footsteps, obey His commandments, talk with Him often, tell others about Him, and share His never-ending love.

Today, Try to Memorize This Verse

This is the day
that the LORD has made.
Let us rejoice and be glad today!

Psalm 118:24 ICB

Here's a Bible verse that you should learn.
Practice saying it several times.
And then, talk to mom or dad
about exactly what the verse means.

When Nobody is Watching

A final word: Be strong with
the Lord's mighty power.
Ephesians 6:10 NLT

When your teachers or parents aren't watching, what should you do? The answer, of course, is that you should behave exactly like you would if they were watching you. But sometimes, you may be tempted to do otherwise.

When a parent steps away or a teacher looks away, you may be tempted to say something or do something that you would not do if they were standing right beside you. But remember this: when nobody's watching, it's up to you to control yourself. And that's exactly what everybody wants you to do: your teachers want you to control yourself, and so do your parents. And so, by the way, does God.

Focus on the Right Things

Keep your eyes focused on what is right.
Keep looking straight ahead to what is good.
Proverbs 4:25 ICB

In the Book of Proverbs, King Solomon gave us wonderful advice for living wisely. Solomon said that we should keep our eyes "focused on what is right." In other words, we should do our best to say and do the things that we know are pleasing to God.

The next time you're tempted to say an unkind word or to say something that isn't true, remember the advice of King Solomon. Solomon knew that it's always better to do the right thing, even when it's tempting to do otherwise. So if you know something is wrong, don't do it; instead, do what you know to be right. When you do, you'll be saving yourself a lot of trouble and you'll be obeying the Word of God.

Today's Tip

Study God's Word each day, and strive to understand God's teachings. Seek to live in accordance with those teachings.

The Kid in the Mirror

For you made us only a little lower than God,
and you crowned us with glory and honor.
Psalm 8:5 NLT

Do you really like the person you see when you look into the mirror? You should! After all, the person in the mirror is a very special person who is made—and loved—by God.

In fact, you are loved in many, many ways: God loves you, your parents love you, and your family loves you, for starters. So you should love yourself, too.

So here's something to think about: since God thinks you're special, and since so many people think you're special, isn't it about time for you to agree with them? Of course, it is! It's time to say, "You're very wonderful and very special," to the person you see in the mirror.

Today's Tip

God loves you . . . and you should too.

You'll Feel Better About Yourself When You Share

The one who blesses others is abundantly blessed; those who help others are helped.
Proverbs 11:25 MSG

The more you share, the quicker you'll discover this fact: Good things happen to people (like you) who are kind enough to share the blessings that God has given them.

Sharing makes you feel better about yourself. Whether you're at home or at school, remember that the best rewards go to the kids who are kind and generous—not to the people who are unkind or stingy. So do what's right: share. You'll feel lots better about yourself when you do.

A Thought for Today

When somebody needs a helping hand, he doesn't need it tomorrow or the next day. He needs it now, and that's exactly when you should offer to help. Good deeds, if they are really good, happen sooner rather than later.

Marie T. Freeman

Parents Know Best!

Success, success to you, and success to those
who help you, for your God will help you....
1 Chronicles 12:18 NIV

God makes this promise: If you have faith
in Him, you can do BIG things! So if you have
something important to do, pray about it and
ask God for help. When you ask God to help
you, He will. And while you're at it, never be
afraid to ask you parents for help.

When you talk things over with your
parents, you'll soon discover that they want
you to do BIG things . . . and they can give you
LOTS of help.

A Thought for Today

Success and happiness are not destinations.
They are exciting, never-ending journeys.
Zig Ziglar

Honesty Has Big Rewards

Tell each other the truth because
we all belong to each other . . . .
Ephesians 4:25 ICB

It's important to be honest. When you tell
the truth, you'll feel better about yourself,
and other people will feel better about you,
too. But that's not all. When you tell the truth,
God knows—and He will reward you for your
honesty.

Telling the truth is hard sometimes. But it's
better to be honest, even when it's hard. So
remember this: telling the truth is always the
right thing to do . . . always.

Today's Tip

White lies? Beware! Sometimes, you're tempted
to "shade" the truth. Unfortunately, little
white lies have a tendency to turn black . . .
and they grow. The best strategy is to avoid
untruths of all sizes and colors.

Today, Try to Memorize This Verse

And what does the LORD
require of you?
To act justly
and to love mercy
and to walk humbly
with your God.

Micah 6:8 NIV

Here's a Bible verse that you should learn.
Practice saying it several times.
And then, talk to mom or dad
about exactly what the verse means.

Honesty Pays

These are the things you must do:
Speak truth to one another; render honest
and peaceful judgments in your gates.

Zechariah 8:16 HCSB

Do you want other people to be honest
with you? Of course you do. And that's why
you should be honest with them. The words of
Matthew 7:12 remind us that, as believers in
Christ, we should treat others as we wish to be
treated. And that means telling them the truth!

The Golden Rule is your tool for deciding
how you will treat other people. When you use
the Golden Rule as your guide for living, your
words and your actions will be pleasing to other
people and to God.

Today's Tip

It is important to treat all people with respect
and kindness.

Big Ideas About . . .

Behaving Yourself

Here are two important ideas.
Take a few minutes to talk to your mom or dad
about what these quotations mean.

Parents can only give good advice or
put them on the right paths,
but the final forming of a person's character
lies in their own hands.

Anne Frank

If we do the wrong thing,
we are quite likely never to know
what we have lost by it.

Laura Ingalls Wilder

Learning To Share

When you do things, do not let selfishness or pride be your guide. Be humble and give more honor to others than to yourselves.

Philippians 2:3 ICB

Lots of people in the world aren't as fortunate as you are. Some of these folks live in faraway places, and that makes it harder to help them. But other people who need your help are living very near you.

Ask your parents to help you find ways to do something nice for folks who need it. And don't forget that everybody needs love, kindness, and respect, so you should always be ready to share those things, too.

A Thought for Today

He climbs highest who helps another up.

Zig Ziglar

Where Does God Fit In?

Every morning he wakes me.
He teaches me to listen like a student.
The Lord God helps me learn...
Isaiah 50:4-5 NCV

Where does God fit in to your life? Do you "squeeze Him in" on Sundays and at mealtimes? Or do you talk to Him more often than that?

Even if you're the busiest kid on the planet, you can still make time for God. And when you think about it, isn't that the very least you should do?

Today's Tip

Find the best time of the day to spend with God: Hudson Taylor, an English Missionary, wrote, "Whatever is your best time in the day, give that to communion with God." That's powerful advice that leads to a powerful faith.

Today, Try to Memorize This Verse

Jesus answered,
"If people love me,
they will obey my teaching.
My Father will love them,
and we will come to them
and make our home with them."

John 14:23 NCV

Here's a Bible verse that you should learn.
Practice saying it several times.
And then, talk to mom or dad
about exactly what the verse means.

Stop Fighting

It's a mark of good character to avert quarrels,
but fools love to pick fights.

Proverbs 20:3 MSG

Since the days of Cain and Abel, people
have discovered plenty of things to fight about
(Cain and Abel, by the way, were the sons
of Adam and Eve). It seems that fighting is a
favorite activity for many people, even though
it's almost always the wrong thing to do.

Kids should do their best to avoid fights,
period. So do yourself a favor: try to avoid
senseless scuffles, foolish fights, alarming
arguments, and constant conflicts. You'll be
glad you did . . . and so will God.

Today's Tip

Tempted to fight? Walk away. The best fights
are those that never happen.

Don't Grow Tired Of Forgiving

Then Peter came to him and asked,
"Lord, how often should I forgive someone
who sins against me? Seven times?"
"No!" Jesus replied, "seventy times seven!"
Matthew 18:21-22 NLT

How often does God forgive us? More times
than we can count! And that, by the way, is
exactly how many times that God expects us to
forgive other people—more times than we care
to count.

Of this you can be sure: God won't ever get
tired of forgiving you. And, because He has
forgiven you, He doesn't want you to get tired
of forgiving other people . . . ever!

Today's Tip

The time to forgive is now! God wants you to
forgive people now, not later. Why? Because
God knows that it's the right thing to do. And,
of course, God wants you to be happy, not
angry. God knows what's best for you, so if you
have somebody you need to forgive, do it now.

Big Ideas About...

Kindness

Here are two important ideas.
Take a few minutes to talk to your mom or dad
about what these quotations mean.

Do all the good you can.
By all the means you can.
In all the ways you can.
In all the places you can.
At all the times you can.
To all the people you can.
As long as ever you can.

John Wesley

The mark of a Christian is that he will walk
the second mile and turn the other cheek.
A wise man or woman gives the extra effort,
all for the glory of the Lord Jesus Christ.

John Maxwell

Real Love

For the LORD your God has arrived
to live among you. He is a mighty savior.
He will rejoice over you with great gladness.
With his love, he will calm all your fears.
He will exult over you by singing a happy song.
Zephaniah 3:17 NLT

How big is God's love for you? As long
as you're alive, you'll never be able to figure
it out because God's love is just too big to
understand. But this much we know: God loves
you so much that He sent His Son Jesus to
come to this earth so you could live forever in
heaven.

God's love is bigger and more powerful than
anybody can imagine, but His love is very real.
So do yourself a favor right now: accept God's
love with open arms and welcome His Son Jesus
into your heart. When you do, your life will be
changed today, tomorrow, and forever.

Today, Try to Memorize This Verse

Guard your heart above all else,
for it is the source of life.

Proverbs 4:23 HCSB

Here's a Bible verse that you should learn.
Practice saying it several times.
And then, talk to mom or dad
about exactly what the verse means.

Promises You Can Trust

Do not be afraid or discouraged.
For the LORD your God is with you
wherever you go.
Joshua 1:9 NLT

God has made quite a few promises to you, and He intends to keep every single one of them. You will find these promises in a book like no other: the Holy Bible. The Bible is your map for life here on earth and for life in heaven.

God's promises never fail and they never grow old. You must trust those promises and share them with your family, with your friends, and with the world . . . starting now . . . and ending never.

Today's Tip

God keeps His promises to you, so make sure that you keep your promises to Him.

God Can Handle It

Now the God of all grace, who called you
to His eternal glory in Christ Jesus,
will personally restore, establish,
strengthen, and support you.

1 Peter 5:10 HCSB

It's a promise that is made over and over again in the Bible: Whatever "it" is, God can handle it.

Life isn't always easy. Far from it! Sometimes, life can be hard, but even then, we're protected by a loving Heavenly Father. When we're worried, God can help us; when we're sad, God can comfort us. God is not just near, He is here. So we should always lift our thoughts and prayers to Him. When we do, He will answer our prayers. Why? Because He is our shepherd, and He has promised to protect us now and forever.

No Secrets

The eyes of the Lord are in every place,
keeping watch . . . .
Proverbs 15:3 NKJV

Even when nobody else is watching, God is. Nothing that we say or do escapes the watchful eye of our Lord. God understands that we are not perfect, but He also wants us to live according to His rules, not our own.

The next time that you're tempted to say something that you shouldn't say or to do something that you shouldn't do, remember that you can't keep secrets from God. So don't even try!

Today's Tip

Having trouble hearing God? If so, slow yourself down, tune out the distractions, and listen carefully. God has important things to say; your task is to be still and listen.

Gossip?

So rid yourselves of all wickedness, all deceit,
hypocrisy, envy, and all slander.

1 Peter 2:1 HCSB

Do you know what gossip is? It's when
we say bad things about people who are not
around. When we gossip, we hurt others and
we hurt ourselves. That's why the Bible tells us
that gossip is wrong.

Sometimes, It's tempting to say bad things
about people, and when we do, it makes us feel
important . . . for a while. But, after a while,
the bad things that we say come back to hurt
us, and of course they hurt other people, too.

So if you want to be a kind person and a
good friend, don't gossip . . . and don't listen to
people who do.

Today's Tip

Don't say something behind someone's back
that you wouldn't say to that person directly.

Being a Good Samaritan

But a Samaritan, as he traveled, came where the man was; and when he saw him, he took pity on him. He went to him and bandaged his wounds, pouring on oil and wine. Then he put the man on his own donkey, took him to an inn and took care of him.

Luke 10:33-34 NIV

Sometimes, we would like to help make the world a better place, but we're not sure how to do it. Jesus told the story of the "Good Samaritan," a man who helped a fellow traveler when no one else would. We, too, should be good Samaritans when we find people who need our help. A good place to start helping other people is at home. And, of course, we should also offer our help at school and at church.

Another way that we can help other people is to pray for them. God always hears our prayers, so we should talk with Him as often as we can. When we do, we're not only doing a wonderful thing for the people we pray for, we're also doing a wonderful thing for ourselves, too.

Today, Try to Memorize This Verse

A new commandment
I give to you,
that you love one another.
John 13:34 NKJV

Here's a Bible verse that you should learn.
Practice saying it several times.
And then, talk to mom or dad
about exactly what the verse means.

Look Before You Leap

Enthusiasm without knowledge is not good.
If you act too quickly,
you might make a mistake.
Proverbs 19:2 NCV

Are you sometimes just a little bit impulsive?
Do you sometimes fail to look before you leap?
If so, God wants you to be a little bit more
careful—or maybe a lot more careful!

The Bible makes it clear: we're supposed to
behave wisely, not carelessly. But sometimes,
we're tempted to rush ahead and do things
before we think about them.

So do yourself a big favor—slow down,
think things through, and look carefully before
you leap.

Today's Tip

No so fast! If you're about to do something,
but you're not sure if it's the right thing to do,
slow down! It's better to make a good decision
than a fast decision.

Thanks For The Memories

I give thanks to my God
for every remembrance of you.
Philippians 1:3 HCSB

In his letter to the Philippians, Paul wrote to his distant friends saying that he thanked God every time he remembered them. We, too, should thank God for the family and friends He has brought into our lives.

Today, let's give thanks to God for all the people who love us, for brothers and sisters, parents and grandparents, aunts and uncles, cousins, and friends. And then, as a way of thanking God, let's obey Him by being especially kind to our loved ones. They deserve it, and so does He.

A Thought for Today

The best times in life are made
a thousand times better
when shared with a dear friend.
Luci Swindoll

Forgiveness Can Be Hard

Anyone who claims to live in God's light and hates a brother or sister is still in the dark.
1 John 2:9 MSG

Sometimes, it's very hard! But God tells us that we must forgive other people, even when we'd rather not. So, if you're angry with anybody (or if you're upset by something you yourself have done) it's time to forgive. Right now!

But what if you have already tried to forgive somebody yet, you simply can't do it? Then you must keep trying. If you can't seem to forgive someone, you should keep asking God to help you until you do. And you can be sure of this: if you keep asking for God's help, He will give it.

Today's Tip

Because God has forgiven you, you can forgive yourself.

God Solves Problems

Since God assured us, "I'll never let you down, never walk off and leave you," we can boldly quote, God is there, ready to help; I'm fearless no matter what. Who or what can get to me?
Hebrews 13:5-6 MSG

Do you have a problem that you haven't been able to solve? Welcome to the club! Life is full of problems that don't have easy solutions. But if you have a problem that you can't solve, there is something you can do: turn that problem over to God. He can handle it.

God has a way of solving our problems if we let Him; our job is to let Him. God can handle things that we can't. And the sooner we turn our concerns over to Him, the sooner He will go to work solving those troubles that are simply too big for us to handle.

If you're worried or discouraged, pray about it. And ask your parents and friends to pray about it, too. And then stop worrying because no problem is too big for God; not even yours.

Think Good Thoughts

Come near to God, and God will come near to
you. You sinners, clean sin out of your lives.
You who are trying to follow God
and the world at the same time,
make your thinking pure.

James 4:8 NCV

Do you try to think good thoughts about
your friends, your family, and yourself? The
Bible says that you should. Do you lift your
hopes and your prayers to God many times each
day? The Bible says that you should. Do you say
"no" to people who want you to do bad things
or think bad thoughts? The Bible says that you
should.

The Bible teaches you to guard your
thoughts against things that are hurtful or
wrong. So remember this: When you turn away
from bad thoughts and turn instead toward
God and His Son Jesus, you will be protected
. . . and you will be blessed.

Trusting God

"I say this because I know what I am planning for you," says the Lord. "I have good plans for you, not plans to hurt you. I will give you hope and a good future."

Jeremiah 29:11 NCV

Sometimes, things happen that we simply don't understand. And that's exactly how God intends it! You see God has given us many gifts, but He hasn't given us the power to understand everything that happens in our world (that comes later, when we get to heaven!)

The Bible tells us God's plans are far bigger than we humans can possibly understand. That's one of the reasons that God doesn't make His plans clear to us. But even when we can't understand why God allows certain things to happen, we can trust His love for us.

The Bible does make one part of God's plan perfectly clear: we should accept His Son Jesus into our hearts so that we might have eternal life (John 3:16). And when we do, we are protected today, tomorrow, and forever.

Telling the Truth

I speak the truth in Christ—I am not lying;
my conscience is testifying to me
with the Holy Spirit.
Romans 9:1 HCSB

Sometimes, telling the truth is hard, but even then, it's easier to tell the truth than it is to live with the consequences of telling a lie. You see, telling a lie can be easier in the beginning, but it's always harder in the end! In the end, when people find out that you've been untruthful, they may feel hurt and you will feel embarrassed.

So make this promise to yourself, and keep it: don't let lies rob you of your happiness. Instead, tell the truth from the start. You'll be doing yourself a big favor, and you'll be obeying the Word of God.

A Thought for Today

Those who walk in truth, walk in liberty.
Beth Moore

Big Ideas About . . .

God's Plans

Here are two important ideas.
Take a few minutes to talk to your mom or dad
about what these quotations mean.

When the dream of our heart is one
that God has planted there, a strange
happiness flows into us. At that moment,
all of the spiritual resources of the universe
are released to help us.

Catherine Marshall

God is at work; He is in full control;
He is in the midst of whatever has happened,
is happening, and will happen.

Charles Swindoll

The Best Day

This is the day the LORD has made.
We will rejoice and be glad in it.
Psalm 118:24 NLT

What is the best day to celebrate life? This one! Today and every day should be a time for celebration as we think about all the things God has done for us.

Today, as you take time to count your blessings, enjoy yourself. This day (like every other one) is a gift from your Heavenly Father . . . SO CELEBRATE!

Today's Tip

While you're celebrating life, don't try and keep the celebration to yourself. Let other people know why you're rejoicing, and don't be bashful about telling them how they can rejoice, too.

What a Friend

And I am convinced that nothing can ever separate us from his love. Whether we are high above the sky or in the deepest ocean, nothing in all creation will ever be able to separate us from the love of God that is revealed in Christ Jesus our Lord.

Romans 8:38–39 NLT

Perhaps you've heard these words before: "Jesus loves me, this I know, for the Bible tells me so." Of course, these words can be found in the song "Jesus Loves Me." It's a wonderful song that should remind you of something very important: Jesus loves you very much.

When you invite Jesus to become your friend, He will do it . . . and He'll be your friend forever. If you make mistakes, He'll still be your friend. If you misbehave, He'll still love you. If you feel sorry or sad, He can help you feel better.

Yes, Jesus loves you more than you know. And when you welcome Him into your heart, you will be blessed now and forever.

Loving Both Friends and Enemies

You have heard that the law of Moses says,
'Love your neighbor' and hate your enemy.
But I say, love your enemies! Pray for those
who persecute you! In that way,
you will be acting as true children of
your Father in heaven.

Matthew 5:43-45 NLT

It's easy to love people who have been nice
to you, but it's very hard to love people who
have treated you badly. Still, Jesus instructs us
to treat both our friends and our enemies with
kindness and respect.

Are you having problems being nice to
someone? Is there someone you know whom you
don't like very much? Remember that Jesus not
only forgave His enemies, He also loved them . . .
and so should you.

Today's Tip

How hard is it to love your enemies? You'll
never know until you try . . . so try!

An Example For Others

In everything you do, stay away from complaining and arguing, so that no one can speak a word of blame against you. You are to live clean, innocent lives as children of God in a dark world full of crooked and perverse people. Let your lives shine brightly before them.

Philippians 2:14-15 NLT

What kind of example are you? Are you the kind of person who shows other people what it means to be kind and forgiving? Hopefully so!

How hard is it to say a kind word? Not very! How hard is it to accept someone's apology? Usually, not too hard. So today, be a good example for others to follow. Because God needs people, like you, who are willing to stand up and be counted for Him. And that's exactly the kind of example you should try to be.

Today's Tip

Your behavior speaks volumes about your relationship with God.

Today, Try to Memorize This Verse

It is good and pleasant
when God's people
live together in peace!

Psalm 133:1 NCV

Here's a Bible verse that you should learn.
Practice saying it several times.
And then, talk to mom or dad
about exactly what the verse means.

A Roadblock

Those who show mercy to others are happy,
because God will show mercy to them.

Matthew 5:7 NCV

If you're unwilling to forgive other people,
you're building a roadblock between yourself
and God. And the less you're willing to forgive,
the bigger your roadblock.

If you really want to forgive someone, pray
for that person. And then pray for yourself by
asking God to help you forgive. Don't expect
forgiveness to be easy or quick, but with God
as your helper, you can forgive . . . and you will.

A Thought for Today

God calls upon the loved not just to love
but to be loving. God calls upon the forgiven
not just to forgive but to be forgiving.

Beth Moore

What A Friend!

But God proves His own love for us in that
while we were still sinners Christ died for us!
Romans 5:8 HCSB

Do you know that Jesus loves you? And
have you thought about exactly what His love
should mean to you? Well, Christ's love should
make you feel better about your life, your
family, your future, and yourself.

There's an old song that says, "What a
friend we have in Jesus." Those words are
certainly true! When you invite Him into your
heart, Jesus will be your friend forever.

Jesus wants you to have a happy, healthy
life. He wants you to behave yourself, and He
wants you to feel good about yourself. And
now, it's up to you to do your best to live up to
the hopes and dreams of your very best friend:
Jesus.

Big Ideas About . . .

Saying Thanks to God

Here are two important ideas.
Take a few minutes to talk to your mom or dad
about what these quotations mean.

Praise and thank God for who He is and for what He has done for you.

Billy Graham

Thank God every morning when you get up that
you have something to do that day which must
be done, whether you like it or not.

Charles Kingsley

Wisdom

Choose my instruction instead of silver,
knowledge rather than choice gold,
for wisdom is more precious than rubies,
and nothing you desire can compare with her.

Proverbs 8:10-11 NIV

If you look in a dictionary, you'll see that the word "wisdom" means "using good judgement, and knowing what is true." But there's more: it's not just enough to know what's right; if you really want to become a wise person, you must also do what's right.

A big part of "doing what's right" is learning self-control . . . and the best day to start learning self-control is this one!

Today's Tip

Need wisdom? Study God's Word and hang out with wise people.

If You're Not Sure What to Do . . .

Listen in silence before me . . . .
Isaiah 41:1 NLT

If you're not certain whether something is right or wrong, ask yourself a simple question: "How would Jesus behave if He were here?" The answer to that question will tell you what to do.

Jesus was perfect, but we are not. Still, we must try as hard as we can to be like Him. When we do, we will love others, just like Christ loves us.

Today's Tip

Want to know what Jesus would do? Then learn what Jesus did!

Anger Strikes Out

A foolish person loses his temper.
But a wise person controls his anger.
Proverbs 29:11 ICB

The Bible tells us that we should control our tempers. But sometimes, especially when we're angry or frustrated, our words and our actions may not be so gentle. Sometimes, we may say things or do things that are unkind or hurtful to others. When we do, we're wrong.

The next time you're tempted to strike out in anger, don't. And if you want to help your family and friends, remember that gentle words are better than harsh words and good deeds are better than the other kind. Always!

Today's Tip

Count to ten . . . but don't stop there! If you're angry with someone, don't say the first thing that comes to your mind. Instead, catch your breath and start counting until you are once again in control of your temper. If you count to a thousand and you're still counting, go to bed! You'll feel better in the morning.

Pay Attention to Your Bible

Every part of Scripture is God-breathed and
useful one way or another, showing us truth,
exposing our rebellion, correcting
our mistakes, training us to live God's way.
Through the Word we are put together
and shaped up for the tasks God has for us.

2 Timothy 3:16-17 MSG

Do you think about the Bible a lot . . . or
not?

Hopefully, you pay careful attention to the
things you learn from God's Word! After all,
the Bible is God's message to you. It's not just a
book, it's a priceless, one-of-a-kind treasure . . .
and it has amazing things to teach you. So start
learning about the Bible now, and keep learning
about it for as long as you live!

Today's Tip

Who's supposed to be taking care of your Bible?
If it's you, then take very good care of it; it's by
far the most important book you own!

Today, Try to Memorize This Verse

Good people's words
will help many others.
Proverbs 10:21 NCV

Here's a Bible verse that you should learn.
Practice saying it several times.
And then, talk to mom or dad
about exactly what the verse means.

Obedience Leads to Happiness

He who seeks good finds goodwill, but evil comes to him who searches for it.
Proverbs 11:27 NIV

Do you want to be happy? Then you should learn to obey your parents and your teachers. And, of course, you should also learn to obey God. When you do, you'll discover that happiness goes hand-in-hand with good behavior.

The happiest people do not misbehave; the happiest people are not cruel or greedy. The happiest people don't disobey their parents, their teachers, or their Father in heaven. The happiest people are those who obey the rules . . . and it's up to you to make sure that you're one of those happy people.

Today's Tip

When should you get tired of obeying God? The answer to that question is simple: Never!

Sometimes It's Good To Be Still

Truly my soul silently waits for God;
from Him comes my salvation.
Psalm 62:1 NKJV

Psalm 37:7 makes it clear that we should "Be still before the Lord and wait patiently for Him" (NIV). But sometimes it's hard to sit still, and sometimes it's even harder to be patient! No matter. God wants us to be patient, and we must obey Him or suffer the consequences.

We should be patient with our families, with our friends, and with ourselves . . . especially with ourselves.

Today's Tip

If you think you're about to say or do something you'll regret later, slow down and take a deep breath, or two deep breaths, or ten, or . . . well you get the idea.

Big Ideas About...

Pleasing God

Here are two important ideas.
Take a few minutes to talk to your mom or dad
about what these quotations mean.

You will get untold flak
for prioritizing God's revealed
and present will for
your life over man's . . .
but, boy, is it worth it.

Beth Moore

Make God's will the focus of your life day by
day. If you seek to please Him and Him alone,
you'll find yourself satisfied with life.

Kay Arthur

Forgive Fast

Mockers can get a whole town agitated,
but those who are wise will calm anger.
Proverbs 29:8 NLT

Today and every day, make sure that you're
a person who is known for the kind way that
you treat everybody. That's how God wants you
to behave.

And if someone says something to you that
isn't very nice, don't pay too much attention.
Just forgive that person as quickly as you can,
and try to move on . . . as quickly as you can.

A Thought for Today

We are all fallen creatures
and all very hard to live with.
C. S. Lewis

Need Something? Pray About It!

For the eyes of the Lord are over
the righteous, and his ears
are open unto their prayers . . . .
1 Peter 3:12 KJV

Would you like to become a more patient person? Then pray about it. Would you like to learn how to use better self-control? Then pray about it. Are you tempted to throw a temper tantrum? Pray about it.

Whenever you pray about something, God hears your prayer . . . and He can help. So don't worry about things; pray about them. God is waiting . . . and listening!

Today's Tip

Even when prayer does not change your circumstances, prayer is essential because it changes you.

Today, Try to Memorize This Verse

In everything set them
an example
by doing what is good.
Titus 2:7 NIV

Here's a Bible verse that you should learn.
Practice saying it several times.
And then, talk to mom or dad
about exactly what the verse means.

Bad Habits?

For every tree is known by its own fruit.
Luke 6:44 NKJV

Perhaps you've tried to become a more disciplined person, but you're still falling back into your old habits. If so, don't get discouraged. Instead, become even more determined to become the person God wants you to be.

If you trust God, and if you keep asking Him to help you change bad habits, He will help you make yourself into a new person. So, if at first you don't succeed, keep praying. If you keep asking, you'll eventually get the answers you need.

Today's Tip

Choose your habits carefully: habits are easier to make than they are to break, so be careful!

Only One You

To acquire wisdom is to love oneself; people who cherish understanding will prosper.
Proverbs 19:8 NLT

How many people in the world are exactly like you? Only one—the person you see every time you look in the mirror. In other words, the only person in the world who's exactly like you . . . IS YOU! And that means you're special: special to God, special to your family, special to your friends, and a special addition to God's wonderful world!

The Bible says that God made you in "an amazing and wonderful way." So, the next time that you start feeling like you don't measure up, remember this: when God made all the people of the earth, He only made one you. And that means you're a V.I.P. And what is a V.I.P.?

A "Very Important Person," of course.

Big Ideas About . . .

God's Love

Here are two important ideas.
Take a few minutes to talk to your mom or dad
about what these quotations mean.

The great love of God is
an ocean without a bottom
or a shore.

C. H. Spurgeon

Though our feelings come and go,
God's love for us does not.

C. S. Lewis

Today, Try to Memorize This Verse

God is our refuge
and strength,
a very present help
in trouble.

Psalm 46:1 NKJV

Here's another important Bible verse that you should learn. Practice saying it several times. And then, talk to mom or dad about exactly what the verse means.

The Truth

Go after a life of love as if your life depended
on it—because it does. Give yourselves to
the gifts God gives you. Most of all,
try to proclaim his truth.

1 Corinthians 14:1 MSG

Jesus had a message for His followers. He
said, "The truth will set you free." When we
do the right thing and tell the truth, we don't
need to worry about our lies catching up with
us. When we behave honestly, we don't have to
worry about feeling guilty or ashamed. But, if
we fail to do what we know is right, bad things
start to happen, and we feel guilty.

Jesus understood that the truth is a very
good thing indeed. We should understand it,
too. And we should keep telling it as long as we
live.

Today's Tip

Don't be satisfied to sit on the sidelines and
observe the truth at a distance—live it.

Your Family Has Rules

This is how we are sure that we have come to know Him: by keeping His commands.
1 John 2:3 HCSB

Face facts: your family has rules . . . rules that you're not supposed to break.

If you're old enough to know right from wrong, then you're old enough to do something about it. In other words, you should always try to obey your family's rules.

How can you tell "the right thing" from "the wrong thing?" By listening carefully to your parents, that's how.

The more self-control you have, the easier it is to obey your parents. Why? Because, when you learn to think first and do things next, you avoid making silly mistakes. So here's what you should do: First, slow down long enough to listen to your parents. Then, do the things that you know your parents want you to do.

Face facts: your family has rules . . . and it's better for everybody when you obey them.

Life Is a Gift

Live full lives, full in the fullness of God.
God can do anything, you know—far more than
you could ever imagine or guess or request in
your wildest dreams! He does it not by pushing
us around but by working within us,
his Spirit deeply and gently within us.

Ephesians 3:19-20 MSG

Life is a gift from God. Your job is to
unwrap that gift, to use it wisely, and to give
thanks to the Giver.

Are you going to treat this day (and every
one hereafter) as a special gift to be enjoyed
and celebrated? You should—and if you really
want to please God, that's exactly what you will
do.

Today's Tip

Slow down to marvel at the beauty of God's
glorious creation.

Everybody Needs to Hear Kind Words

Avoid irreverent, empty speech,
for this will produce an even greater measure
of godlessness.

2 Timothy 2:16 HCSB

Your words can help people . . . or not.
Make certain that you're the kind of person
who says helpful things, not hurtful things.
You'll feel better about yourself when you help
other people feel better about themselves.

Do you like for people to say kind words
to you? Of course you do! And that's exactly
how other people feel, too. That's why it's so
important to say things that make people feel
better, not worse.

Everybody needs to hear kind words, and
that's exactly the kind of words they should
hear from you!

Today's Tip

If you don't know what to say . . . don't say
anything. Sometimes, a hug works better than a
whole mouthful of words.

Big Ideas About . . .

Putting Things Off Until the Last Minute

Here are two important ideas.
Take a few minutes to talk to your mom or dad
about what these quotations mean.

Now is the only time worth
having because, indeed,
it is the only time we have.

C. H. Spurgeon

Every time you refuse to face up to life
and its problems, you weaken your character.

E. Stanley Jones

Sharing at Home

Whoever does not care for his own relatives,
especially his own family members, has turned
against the faith and is worse than someone
who does not believe in God.

1 Timothy 5:8 NCV

A good place to start sharing is at home—
but it isn't always an easy place to start.
Sometimes, especially when we're tired or mad,
we don't treat our family members as nicely as
we should. And that's too bad!

Do you have brothers and sisters or
cousins? If so, you're lucky.

Sharing your things—without whining or
complaining—is a wonderful way to show your
family that you love them. So the next time
a brother or sister or cousin asks to borrow
something, say "yes" without getting mad. It's a
great way to say, "I love you."

A Thought for Today

What is your focus today? Joy comes when
it is Jesus first, others second...then you.

Kay Arthur

Your Amazing Talents!

There are diversities of gifts,
but the same Spirit.
1 Corinthians 12:4 NKJV

Face the facts: you've got very special talents, talents that have been given to you by God. So here's a question: will you use your talents or not? God wants you to use your talents to become a better person and a better Christian. And that's what you should want for yourself.

As you're trying to figure out exactly what you're good at, be sure and talk about it with your parents. They can help you decide how best to use and improve the gifts God has given you.

Today's Tip

God gives you talents for a reason: to use them.

Directing Your Thoughts!

And now, dear brothers and sisters, let me say one more thing as I close this letter. Fix your thoughts on what is true and honorable and right. Think about things that are pure and lovely and admirable. Think about things that are excellent and worthy of praise.

Philippians 4:8 NLT

Do you direct your thoughts toward things that are honorable, true, and uplifting? The Bible says that you should. Do you lift your hopes and your prayers to God many times each day? The Bible says that you should. Do you turn away from bad thoughts and bad people? The Bible says that you should.

The Bible instructs you to guard your thoughts against things that are hurtful or wrong. And when you turn away from the bad and turn instead toward God and His Son Jesus, you will be protected and you will be blessed.

Lessons You Can Learn

Remember what you are taught.
And listen carefully to words of knowledge.
Proverbs 23:12 ICB

You can learn a lot about life by paying attention to the things that happen around you . . . and that's exactly what God wants you to do. God is trying to teach you things, and you can learn those things the easy way (by paying attention and obeying God's rules) or the hard way (by making the same mistakes over and over again until you finally learn something from them). Of course, it's better to learn things sooner rather than later . . . starting now.

A Thought for Today

While it is wise to learn from experience, it is wiser to learn from the experience of others.
Rick Warren

Real Faith

I've laid down a pattern for you.
What I've done, you do.
John 13:15 MSG

Jesus wants to have a real relationship with you. Are you willing to have a radical relationship with Him? Unless you can answer this question with a resounding "Yes," you may miss out on some wonderful things.

This day offers yet another opportunity to behave yourself like a real Christian. When you do, God will guide your steps and bless your endeavors . . . forever.

Today's Tip

If you want to be a little more like Christ . . . learn about His teachings, follow in His footsteps, and obey His commandments.

A Pure Heart

For the word of God is living and active.
Sharper than any double-edged sword,
it penetrates even to dividing soul and spirit,
joints and marrow; it judges the thoughts
and attitudes of the heart.

Hebrews 4:12 NIV

Where does a good attitude begin? It starts in our hearts and works its way out from there. Jesus taught us that a pure heart is a wonderful blessing. It's up to each of us to fill our hearts with love for God, love for Jesus, and love for all people. When we do, good things happen.

Sometimes, of course, we don't feel much like feeling good. Sometimes, when we're tired, or frustrated, or angry, we simply don't want to have a good attitude. On those days when we're feeling bad, it's time to calm down . . . and rest up.

Do you want to be the best person you can be? Then you shouldn't grow tired of doing the right things . . . and you shouldn't ever grow tired of thinking the right thoughts.

Inside Out

God does not see the same way people see.
People look at the outside of a person,
but the Lord looks at the heart.

1 Samuel 16:7 NCV

Other people see you from the outside, and sometimes people will judge you by the way you look. But God doesn't care how you look on the outside. Why? Because God is wiser than that; God cares about who you are on the inside—God sees your heart.

If you're like most people, you worry a little bit about the way you look (or maybe you worry a lot about it). But please don't worry too much about your appearance!

How you look on the outside isn't important . . . but how you feel on the inside is important. So don't worry about trying to impress other people. Instead of trying to impress other kids, try to impress God by being the best person you can be.

Choices Matter

The thing you should want most is God's
kingdom and doing what God wants.
Then all these other things you need
will be given to you.

Matthew 6:33 NCV

There's really no way to get around it:
choices matter. If you make good choices,
good things will usually happen to you. And if
you make bad choices, bad things will usually
happen.

The next time you have an important
choice to make, ask yourself this: "Am I doing
what God wants me to do?" If you can answer
that question with a great big "YES," then go
ahead. But if you're not sure if the choice you
are about to make is right, slow down. Why?
Because choices matter . . . a lot!

Today's Tip

First you make choices . . . and pretty soon
those choices begin to shape your life. That's
why you must make smart choices . . . or face
the consequences of making dumb ones.

Safety Matters

The prudent see danger and take refuge,
but the simple keep going and suffer from it.
Proverbs 27:12 NIV

Self-control and safety go hand in hand.
Why? Because a big part of self-control is
looking around and thinking things through
before you do something that you might regret
later.

Remember the saying "Look before you
leap?" Well if you want to live safely and happily,
you should look very carefully before you
decide whether or not to leap. After all, it's
easy to leap, but once you're in the middle of
your jump, it's too late to leap back!

Today's Tip

Don't complain about safety: whether it's a
fire drill at school or wearing seat belts in the
family car, don't whine, complain, or resist.
When grown-ups are trying to keep you safe,
your job is to help them do it!

Big Ideas About . . .

Mistakes

Here are two important ideas.
Take a few minutes to talk to your mom or dad
about what these quotations mean.

We become a failure when
we allow mistakes to take away
our ability to learn, give,
grow, and try again.

Susan Lenzkes

When we focus on God, the scene changes.
He's in control of our lives; nothing lies
outside the realm of His redemptive grace.
Even when we make mistakes, fail in
relationships, or deliberately make
bad choices, God can redeem us.

Penelope J. Stokes

Today, Try to Memorize This Verse

A foolish person
enjoys doing wrong,
but a person with understanding
enjoys doing what is wise.

Proverbs 10:23 NCV

Here's a Bible verse that you should learn.
Practice saying it several times.
And then, talk to mom or dad
about exactly what the verse means.

Keep On Forgiving

You have heard that it was said,
"Love your neighbor and hate your enemies."
But I say to you, love your enemies.
Pray for those who hurt you.

Matthew 5:43–44 NCV

If you forgive somebody once, that's enough, right? WRONG!!! Even if you've forgiven somebody many times before, you must keep on forgiving.

Jesus teaches us that we must keep forgiving people even if they continue to misbehave. Why? Because we, too, need to be forgiven, over and over again. And if God keeps forgiving us, then we must be willing to do the same thing for others.

A Thought for Today

If Jesus forgave those who nailed Him to the Cross, and if God forgives you and me, how can you withhold your forgiveness from someone else?

Anne Graham Lotz

Friends You Can Trust

Friends come and friends go,
but a true friend sticks by you like family.
Proverbs 18:24 MSG

All lasting friendships are built upon both honesty and trust. Without trust, friends soon drift apart. But with trust, friends can stay friends for a lifetime.

As Christians, we should always try to be trustworthy friends. And, we should be thankful for the people who are loyal friends to us. When we treat other people with honesty and respect, we not only make more friends, but we also keep the friendships we've already made.

Do you want friends you can trust? Then start by being a friend they can trust. That's the way to make your friendships strong, stronger, and strongest!

Today's Tip

You make friends by being a friend. And when you choose your friends, choose wisely.

Don't Judge!

Don't pick on people, jump on their failures,
criticize their faults—unless, of course,
you want the same treatment.
That critical spirit has a way of boomeranging.
Matthew 7:1-2 MSG

Here's something worth thinking about: If
you judge other people harshly, God will judge
you in the same way. But that's not all (thank
goodness!) The Bible also promises that if you
forgive other people, you, too, will be forgiven.

Are you tempted to blame people, criticize
people, or judge people? If so, remember this:
God is already judging what people do, and He
doesn't need—or want—your help.

Today's Tip

The ability to judge others requires a divine
insight that you simply don't have.

Two Ears and One Mouth

Answering before listening is both
stupid and rude.
Proverbs 18:13 MSG

When God made you, he gave you two ears and one mouth for a very good reason: you can learn at least twice as much by listening as you can by talking. That's why it's usually better to listen first and talk second. But when you're frustrated or tired, it's easy to speak first and think later.

A big part of growing up is learning how to slow down long enough to listen to the things that people have to say. So the next time you're tempted to turn off your ears and tune up your mouth, stop, listen, and think. After all, God gave you two wonderful ears for a very good reason: to use them.

Today's Tip

Try to listen as much (or more) than you speak.

Big Ideas About ...

Prayer

Here are two important ideas.
Take a few minutes to talk to your mom or dad
about what these quotations mean.

Don't be overwhelmed...
take it one day
and one prayer at a time.

Stormie Omartian

Just as our faith strengthens our prayer life,
so do our prayers deepen our faith.
Let us pray often, starting today,
for a deeper, more powerful faith.

Shirley Dobson

Obeying Your Parents

Children, obey your parents in everything,
for this is pleasing in the Lord.
Colossians 3:20 HCSB

When your parents ask you to do something, do you usually obey them or do you usually ignore them? When your parents try to get your attention, do you listen or not? When your parents make rules, do you obey those rules or do you break them? Hopefully, you've learned to listen to your parents and to obey.

In order to be an obedient person, you must first learn how to control yourself—otherwise, you won't be able to behave yourself even if you want to. Controlling yourself means that you must slow down long enough to listen to your parents, and then you must be willing to do something about the things your parents tell you to do.

When you learn the importance of obedience, you'll soon discover that good things happen when you behave yourself. And the sooner you learn to listen and obey, the sooner those good things will start happening . . . to you!

Anger Leads to Trouble

Patience is better than strength.
Proverbs 16:32 ICB

In the Book of Proverbs, King Solomon gave us wonderful advice for living wisely. Solomon warned that impatience and anger lead only to trouble. And he was right!

The next time you're tempted to say an unkind word or to throw a temper tantrum, remember Solomon. He was one of the wisest men who ever lived, and he knew that it's always better to be patient. So remain calm and remember that patience is best. After all, if it's good enough for a wise man like Solomon, it should be good enough for us, too.

Today's Tip

God and your parents have been patient with you . . . now it's your turn to be patient with others.

Pleasing God!

For am I now trying to win the favor of people,
or God? Or am I striving to please people?
If I were still trying to please people,
I would not be a slave of Christ.

Galatians 1:10 HCSB

Are you a people-pleaser or a God-pleaser?
Hopefully, you're far more concerned with
pleasing God than you are with pleasing your
friends. But face the facts: even if you're a
devoted Christian, you're still going to feel the
urge to impress your friends—and sometimes
that urge will be strong.

Here's your choice: you can choose to
please God first, or you can fall victim to peer
pressure. The choice is yours—and so are the
consequences.

Today's Tip

Make up your mind to become friends with
people who encourage you to become a better
person.

If You Think You Can

For though a righteous man falls seven times,
he rises again....
Proverbs 24:16 NIV

If you think you can do something, then you
can probably do it. If you think you can't do
something, then you probably won't do it.

So remember this: if you're having a little
trouble getting something done, don't get mad,
don't get frustrated, don't get discouraged,
and don't give up. Just keep trying . . . and
believe in yourself.

When you try hard—and keep trying hard—
you can really do amazing things . . . but if you
quit at the first sign of trouble, you'll miss out.
So here's a good rule to follow: when you have
something that you want to finish, finish it . . .
and finish it sooner rather than later.

Today's Tip

The next time you find your courage tested
to the limit, remember that God is as near as
your next breath, and remember that He offers
strength and comfort to His children.

Having Trouble Behaving Yourself? Pray About It!

Every man's way is right in his own eyes,
but the LORD weighs the hearts.

Proverbs 21:2 NASB

Do you really want to become a more obedient person? Then pray about it. Would you like to learn how to behave yourself a little bit better? Then pray about it. Want to be able to think about things before you get into trouble, not after? Pray for God's help.

If you have questions about whether you should do something or not, pray about it. If there is something you're worried about, ask God to comfort you. And as you pray more, you'll discover that God is always near and that He's always ready to hear from you. So don't worry about things; pray about them. God is waiting to hear from you . . . so what are you waiting for?

Questions?

In thee, O Lord, do I put my trust;
let me never be put into confusion.

Psalm 71:1 KJV

God doesn't explain Himself to us with the clarity that we humans would prefer (think about this: if God did explain Himself with perfect clarity, we wouldn't have enough brainpower to understand the explanation that He gave!)

When innocent people are hurt, we question God because we can't figure out exactly what He's doing, or why. Since we can't fully answer that question now, we must trust in God's love, God's wisdom, and God's plan.

And while we're waiting for that wonderful day when all our questions will be answered (in heaven), we should use the time that we have here on earth to help the people who need it most.

Sometimes Sad

Those people who know they have great spiritual needs are happy, because the kingdom of heaven belongs to them. Those who are sad now are happy, because God will comfort them.

Matthew 5:3-4 NCV

Sometimes, you feel happy, and sometimes you don't. When you're feeling sad, here are two very important things you should do:

1. Talk to your parents about your feelings.
2. Talk to God about your feelings.

Talking with your parents is helpful because your mom and dad understand this: The problems that seem VERY BIG to you today probably won't seem so big tomorrow.

Talking with God helps because God hears your prayers and He helps make things better.

So the next time you're sad, don't hold your feelings inside—talk things over with your parents and with God. When you do, you'll feel better . . . and so will they!

Big Ideas About...

Forgiveness

Here are two important ideas.
Take a few minutes to talk to your mom or dad
about what these quotations mean.

God specializes in giving people a fresh start.

Rick Warren

There are some facts that will never change.
One fact is that you are forgiven. He sees you
better than you see yourself. And that is a
glorious fact of your life.

Max Lucado

The Choice to Rejoice

Shout with joy to the LORD, O earth!
Worship the LORD with gladness.
Come before him, singing with joy.

Psalm 100:1-2 NLT

Have you made the choice to rejoice? Hopefully so. After all, if you're a Christian, you have plenty of reasons to be joyful.

So today, think about this: God has given you too many blessings to count, but you can certainly count some of those blessings. Your job is to honor God with your prayers, your words, your behavior, and your joy.

A Thought for Today

According to Jesus, it is God's will that His children be filled with the joy of life.

Catherine Marshall

The Best Time to Praise God

The LORD is my strength and song,
and He has become my salvation;
He is my God, and I will praise Him.

Exodus 15:2 NIV

When is the best time to praise God? In church? Before dinner is served? When we tuck little children into bed? None of the above. The best time to praise God is all day, every day, to the greatest extent we can, with thanksgiving in our hearts, and with a song on our lips. Dr. Wayne Oates once admitted, "Many of my prayers are made with my eyes open. You see, it seems I'm always praying about something, and it's not always convenient—or safe—to close my eyes." Dr. Oates understood that God always hears our prayers and that the position of our eyelids is of no concern to Him.

Today, find a little more time to lift your concerns to God in prayer, and praise Him for all that He has done. Whether your eyes are open or closed, He's listening.

Always Tell the Truth

Don't lie to one another. You're done with that old life. It's like a filthy set of ill-fitting clothes you've stripped off and put in the fire. Now you're dressed in a new wardrobe. Every item of your new way of life is custom-made by the Creator, with his label on it. All the old fashions are now obsolete.

Colossians 3:9-10 MSG

Sometimes people lie, and sometimes they get away with it. But that doesn't mean that it's wise to lie. And that doesn't make lying the right thing to do. Far from it.

Whatever the problem, lying is always a bad solution. And, besides, lying is always against the will of God. So even if other people lie, don't ever believe that they have lied successfully. There's no such thing as a successful lie.

A Thought for Today

An honest heart is the first blessing. A knowing heart is the second.

Thomas Jefferson

Big Rewards When You Do the Right Thing

God chose you to be his people, so I urge you now to live the life to which God called you.

Ephesians 4:1 NCV

If you open up a dictionary, you'll see that the word "wisdom" means "using good judgement, and knowing what is true." But there's more to it than that. It's not enough to know what's right—if you want to be wise, you must also do what's right.

The Bible promises that when you do smart things, you'll earn big rewards, so slow down and think about things before you do them, not after.

Today's Tip

Learning about God's truth is "head knowledge" and it is incomplete. Learning and doing God's truth is "head-and-heart knowledge" . . . and it is complete.

Lies Will Lead to Trouble

If you respect the Lord, you will also hate evil.
I hate pride and bragging, evil ways and lies.
Proverbs 8:13 NCV

When we tell a lie, trouble starts. Lots of trouble. But when we tell the truth—and nothing but the truth—we stop Old Man Trouble in his tracks.

When we always tell the truth, we make our worries smaller, not bigger. And that's precisely what God wants us to do.

So, if you'd like to have fewer worries and more happiness, abide by this simple rule: tell the truth, the whole truth, and nothing but the truth. When you do, you'll make many of your worries disappear altogether. And that's the truth!

A Thought for Today

Having truth decay?
Brush up on your Bible!
Anonymous

Thanking Those Who Serve

There are different kinds of gifts, but they are all from the same Spirit. There are different ways to serve but the same Lord to serve.

1 Corinthians 12:4–5 NCV

Jesus instructed His disciples to help each other. Those instructions still apply. If we are to be obedient servants of Christ, we must be willing to help those who can't help themselves. In other words, we must become "servants to all."

Some people choose careers that allow them to serve and protect our homes and our world (this includes police officers, firefighters, and those who serve in our military). These brave men and women make very big sacrifices, and we should thank them whenever we can.

So let's all offer prayers of thanks for those brave men and women who serve and protect us . . . and let's all do our best to serve other people wherever we can.

Big Ideas About . . .

Doing the Right Thing

Here are two important ideas.
Take a few minutes to talk to your mom or dad
about what these quotations mean.

If we have the true love of God in our hearts,
we will show it in our lives. We will not have to
go up and down the earth proclaiming it.
We will show it in everything we say or do.

D. L. Moody

Nobody is good by accident.

C. H. Spurgeon

When Things Go Wrong

We must not become tired of doing good.
Galatians 6:2 ICB

When things don't turn out right, it's easy for most of us to give up. But usually, it's wrong. Why are we tempted to give up so quickly? Perhaps, it's because we're afraid that we might embarrass ourselves if we tried hard but didn't succeed.

Here's something to remember: if you're having a little trouble getting something done, don't get mad, don't get frustrated, don't get discouraged, and don't give up. Just keep trying . . . and keep believing in yourself.

When you try hard—and keep trying hard—you can do amazing things . . . but if you quit at the first sign of trouble, you'll miss out. So here's a good rule to follow: when you have something that you want to finish, be brave enough (and wise enough) to finish it . . . you'll feel better about yourself when you do.

It's a Blessing to Share

God has given gifts to each of you from
his great variety of spiritual gifts.
Manage them well so that God's generosity
can flow through you.

1 Peter 4:10 NLT

Jesus said, "It is more blessed to give than
to receive." That means that we should be
generous with other people—but sometimes, we
don't feel much like sharing. Instead of sharing
the things that we have, we want to keep them
all to ourselves. That's when we must remember
that God doesn't want selfishness to rule our
hearts; He wants us to be generous.

Are you lucky enough to have nice things?
If so, God's instructions are clear: you must
share your blessings with others. And that's
exactly the way it should be. After all, think
about how generous God has been with you.

When We Don't Understand

Immediately the father of the child cried out
and said with tears,
"Lord, I believe; help my unbelief!"
Mark 9:24 NKJV

Even a good man like Moses couldn't always understand the mysteries of God's plans. And neither can we. Sometimes, people who do nothing wrong get sick; sometimes, innocent people are hurt; sometimes, bad things happen to very good people. And just like Moses, we can't always understand why.

But the good news is this: We will have an eternity to have all our questions answered when we get to heaven. And until then, we've simply got to trust God.

Today's Tip

If you're afraid to raise your hand and ask a question, remember this . . . if you don't understand something, lots of other people in the classroom probably don't understand it, either. So you'll be doing everybody a big favor if you raise your hand and ask questions.

Giving to Your Church

Serve the Lord with gladness.
Psalm 100:2 HCSB

When the offering plate passes by, are you old enough to drop anything in it? If you are, congratulations! But if you're not quite old enough to give money to the church, don't worry—there are still lots of things you can share!

Even when you don't have money to share, you still have much to give to your church. What are some things you can share? Well, you can share your smile, your happiness, your laughter, your energy, your cooperation, your prayers, your obedience, your example, and your love.

So don't worry about giving to the church: even if you don't have lots of money, there are still plenty of ways you can give. And the best time to start giving is NOW!

The Right Thing

Because you have these blessings, do your best to add these things to your lives: to your faith, add goodness; and to your goodness, add knowledge; and to your knowledge, add self-control; and to your self-control, add patience; and to your patience, add service for God; and to your service for God, add kindness for your brothers and sisters in Christ; and to this kindness, add love.

2 Peter 1:5-7 NCV

Doing the right thing is not always easy, especially when we're tired or frustrated. But, doing the wrong thing almost always leads to trouble. And sometimes, it leads to BIG trouble.

When you do the right thing, you don't have to worry about what you did or what you said. But, if you are dishonest—or if you do something that you know is wrong—you'll be worried that someone will find out. So do the right thing; it may be harder in the beginning, but it's easier in the end.

Big Ideas About...

Being Joyful

Here are two important ideas.
Take a few minutes to talk to your mom or dad
about what these quotations mean.

The joy of the Holy Spirit is experienced by giving thanks in all situations.

Bill Bright

Our sense of joy, satisfaction,
and fulfillment in life increases,
no matter what the circumstances,
if we are in the center of God's will.

Billy Graham

Who Controls You?

Be imitators of God, therefore,
as dearly loved children.

Ephesians 5:1 NIV

Do you try hard to control yourself? If so, that's good because God wants all His children (including you) to behave themselves.

Sometimes, it's hard to be a well-behaved person, especially if you have friends who don't behave nicely. But if your friends misbehave, don't imitate them. Instead, listen to your conscience, talk to your parents, and do the right thing . . . NOW!

Today's Tip

Start now! If you really want to become a well-behaved person, the best day to get started is this one.

Today, Try to Memorize This Verse

God loves a cheerful giver.

2 Corinthians 9:7 NIV

Here's a Bible verse that you should learn.
Practice saying it several times.
And then, talk to mom or dad
about exactly what the verse means.

Listen to Your Conscience

I always do my best to have a clear conscience
toward God and men.
Acts 24:16 HCSB

Your conscience is a little feeling that will
usually tell you what to do and when to do it.
Pay attention to that feeling, and trust it.

If you slow down and listen to your
conscience, you'll usually stay out of trouble.
And if you listen to your conscience, it won't
be so hard to control your own behavior. Why?
Because most of the time, your conscience
already knows right from wrong. So don't be in
such a hurry to do things. Instead of "jumping
right in," listen to your conscience. In the end,
you'll be very glad you did.

Today's Tip

If you're not sure what to do . . . slow down
and listen to your conscience. That little voice
inside your head is remarkably dependable, but
you can't depend upon it if you never listen to
it. So stop, listen, and learn—your conscience
is almost always right.

See The Good In Others

See to it that no one repays evil for evil to
anyone, but always pursue what is good
for one another and for all.

1 Thessalonians 5:15 HCSB

Do you ever make mistakes? Of course, you
do! Even if you're a very good person, you're
bound to make a mistake or two—everybody
does.

When you do something you shouldn't have
done, here are some things you can do:

1. Apologize to the people you've hurt,
and ask for their forgiveness; 2. Fix the things
you've messed up or broken; 3. Don't make
the same mistake again; 4. Ask God for His
forgiveness (which, by the way, He will give
to you instantly); 5. Get busy doing something
you can be proud of. 6. Don't be too hard on
yourself . . . even if you made a mistake, you're
still a very, very special person!

Slow Down!

Knowing God leads to self-control.
Self-control leads to patient endurance,
and patient endurance leads to godliness.

2 Peter 1:6 NLT

Maybe you're one of those people who try
to do everything fast, faster, or fastest! If so,
maybe you sometimes do things before you
think about the consequences of your actions.
If that's the case, it's probably a good idea to
slow down a little bit so you can think before
you act. When you do, you'll soon discover the
value of thinking carefully about things before
you get started. And while you're at it, it's
probably a good idea to think before you speak,
too. After all, you'll never have to apologize for
something that you didn't say.

A Thought for Today

Discipline is training that develops
and corrects.

Charles Stanley

Today, Try to Memorize This Verse

Do to others
what you want them
to do to you.
Matthew 7:12 NCV

Here's a Bible verse that you should learn.
Practice saying it several times.
And then, talk to mom or dad
about exactly what the verse means.

Listen To God

Continue to ask, and God will give to you.
Continue to search, and you will find.
Continue to knock, and the door
will open for you.

Matthew 7:7 ICB

God has many things He wants to tell us. And for starters, He wants us to be loving, kind, and patient, not rude or mean!

The Bible tells us that God is love and that if we wish to know Him, we must have love in our hearts. Sometimes, of course, when we're tired, angry, or frustrated, it is very hard for us to be loving. Thankfully, anger and frustration are feelings that come and go, but God's love lasts forever.

If you'd like to become a more patient person, talk to God in prayer, listen to what He says, and share His love with your family and friends. God is always listening, and He's ready to talk to you . . . now!

Upset or Worried? Pray About It!

Therefore I want the men in every place to
pray, lifting up holy hands without
anger or argument.

1 Timothy 2:8 HCSB

If you're feeling upset, what should you
do? Well, you should talk to your parents and
there's something else you can do: you can pray
about it.

If there is person you don't like, you should
pray for a forgiving heart. If there is something
you're worried about, you should ask God to
give you comfort. And as you pray more, you'll
discover that God is always near and that He's
always ready to hear from you. So don't worry
about things; pray about them. God is waiting
patiently to hear from you . . . and He's ready
to listen NOW!

Today's Tip

One way to make sure that your heart is in tune
with God is to pray often. The more you talk to
God, the more He will talk to you.

Golden Rule

Don't be selfish . . . . Be humble, thinking of others as better than yourself.

Philippians 2:3 TLB

Some rules are easier to understand than they are to live by. Jesus told us that we should treat other people in the same way that we would want to be treated: that's the Golden Rule. But sometimes, especially when we're tired or upset, that rule is very hard to follow.

Jesus wants us to treat other people with respect, kindness, courtesy, and love. When we do, we make our families and friends happy . . . and we make our Father in heaven very proud.

A Thought for Today

The Golden Rule starts at home, but it should never stop there.

Marie T. Freeman

The Wonder Of Heaven

Be glad and rejoice, because your reward
is great in heaven.

Matthew 5:12 HCSB

The Bible makes this important promise:
when you give your heart to Jesus, you will live
forever with Him in heaven. And Jesus told us
that His house has "many mansions" (John 14:
1-3).

Even though we don't know everything
about heaven, we do know this: heaven will be
a wonderful place, a place of joy and wonder, a
place where we will be reunited with our loved
ones and with God. It's wonderful to think
about . . . and a priceless gift from God.

A Thought for Today

The main joy of heaven will be the heavenly
Father greeting us in a time and place of
rejoicing, celebration, joy, and great reunion.

Bill Bright

Big Ideas About...

Serving Other People

Here are two important ideas.
Take a few minutes to talk to your mom or dad
about what these quotations mean.

God will open up places of service for you
as He sees you are ready. Meanwhile,
study the Bible and give yourself
a chance to grow.

Warren Wiersbe

Carve your name on hearts, not on marble.

C. H. Spurgeon

When Other People Make Mistakes

Be gentle with one another, sensitive.
Forgive one another as quickly and thoroughly
as God in Christ forgave you.

Ephesians 4:32 MSG

When other people make mistakes, you must find a way to forgive them. And when you make mistakes, as you will from time to time, you must hope that other people will forgive you, too.

When you have done things that you regret, you should apologize, you should clean up the mess you've made, you should learn from your mistakes, and—last but not least—you should forgive yourself. Mistakes happen . . . it's simply a fact of life, and it's simply a part of growing up. So don't be too hard on yourself, especially if you've learned something along the way.

A Thought for Today

Father, take our mistakes
and turn them into opportunities.

Max Lucado

Keep Your Eye Upon the Donut

Consider it pure joy, my brothers,
whenever you face trials of many kinds,
because you know that the testing of
your faith develops perseverance.

James 1:2-3 NIV

Here's a poem that was seen many years ago in a small donut shop:

As you travel through life brother, Whatever be your goal, Keep your eye upon the donut, And not upon the hole.

What do you think these words mean? Well, this little poem can teach you an important lesson: You should spend more time looking at the things you have, not worrying about the things you don't have.

When you think about it, you've got more blessings than you can count. So make it a habit to thank God for the gifts He's given you, and don't feel jealous, angry, or sad about all the other stuff.

Making Other People Feel Better

Be gracious in your speech. The goal is to bring
out the best in others in a conversation,
not put them down, not cut them out.

Colossians 4:6 MSG

Do you like for people to say kind words
to you? Of course you do! And that's exactly
how other people feel, too. That's why it's so
important to say things that make people feel
better, not worse.

Your words can help people . . . or not.
Make certain that you're the kind of person
who says helpful things, not hurtful things.
And, make sure that you're the kind of person
who helps other people feel better about
themselves, not worse.

Today's Tip

When in doubt, use the Golden Rule to help
you decide what to say: If you wouldn't like for
somebody to say it about you, don't say it about
them!

When to Stop Temper Tantrums

A hot-tempered person starts fights
and gets into all kinds of sin.
Proverbs 29:22 NLT

Temper tantrums are one of the silliest ways to lose self-control. Why? Because when we lose our temper, we say things that we shouldn't say, and we do things that we shouldn't do. And to make matters worse, once the tantrum is over, we usually feel embarrassed or worse.

The Bible tells us that it isn't very smart to become angry. That's why we should learn to stop temper tantrums before they get started.

A Thought for Today

Imagine your anger to be a kind of wild beast . . . because it too has ferocious teeth and claws, and if you don't tame it, it will devastate all things . . . It not only hurts the body; it even corrupts the health of the soul, devouring, rending, tearing to pieces all its strength, and making it useless for everything.
St. John Chrysostom

Happy Thoughts

Those who are pure in their thinking are happy, because they will be with God.

Matthew 5:8 NCV

Do you try to think the kind of thoughts that make you happy, not sad? The Bible says that you should.

Do you try to think about things that are true and right? The Bible says that you should.

Do you turn away from bad thoughts—and away from people who misbehave? The Bible says that you should.

The Bible instructs you to guard your thoughts against things that are hurtful or wrong. So remember this: when you turn away from the bad thoughts and bad people, you've made a very wise choice.

Today's Tip

It is important to focus your thoughts on the positive aspects of life, not the negative ones.

Contentment Now

*I have learned to be content
in whatever circumstances I am.*
Philippians 4:11 HCSB

Where can we find contentment? Is it a result of being wealthy or famous? Nope. Genuine contentment is a gift from God to those who trust Him and follow His commandments.

If we don't find contentment in God, we will never find it anywhere else. But, if we seek Him and obey Him, we will be blessed with joyful, peaceful, meaningful lives. When God dwells at the center of our lives, peace and contentment will belong to us just as surely as we belong to God.

Today's Tip

Be contented where you are, even if it's not exactly where you want to end up. Think about it like this: God has something wonderful in store for you—and remember that God's timing is perfect—so be patient, trust God, do your best, and expect the best.

The Good Shepherd's Love

I am the good shepherd.
The good shepherd lays down his life
for the sheep.
John 10:11 NIV

You've probably heard the song, "Jesus Loves Me." And exactly how much does He love you? He loves you so much that He gave His life so that you might live forever with Him in heaven.

How can you repay Christ's love? By accepting Him into your heart and by obeying His rules. When you do, He will love you and bless you today, tomorrow, and forever.

A Thought for Today

Jesus is all compassion. He never betrays us.
Catherine Marshall

When Kids Are Unkind

It is God's desire that by doing good you should stop foolish people from saying stupid things about you. Live as free people, but do not use your freedom as an excuse to do evil. Live as servants of God.

1 Peter 2:15-16 NCV

Sometimes, young people can be very mean. They can make fun of other people, and when they do so, it's wrong. Period.

As Christians, we should be kind to everyone. And, if other kids say unkind things to a child or make fun of him or her, it's up to us to step in, like the Good Samaritan, and lend a helping hand.

Today and every day, be a person who is known for your kindness, not for your cruelty. That's how God wants you to behave. Period.

Hit A Homerun

Don't be afraid. Only believe.
Mark 5:36 HCSB

His fans called him the "Sultan of Swat."
He was Babe Ruth, the baseball player who set
records for home runs and strikeouts. Babe's
philosophy was simple. He said, "Never let the
fear of striking out get in your way." That's
smart advice on the diamond or off.

Of course, it's never wise to take foolish
risks (so buckle up, slow down, and don't do
anything stupid!) But when it comes to the
game of life, you should not let the fear of
failure keep you from taking your swings.

A Thought for Today

Success or failure can be pretty well predicted
by the degree to which the heart is fully in it.
John Eldredge

In His Footsteps

Whoever serves me must follow me.
Then my servant will be with me everywhere
I am. My Father will honor anyone
who serves me.

John 12:26 NCV

Jesus walks with you. Are you walking with Him? Hopefully, you will choose to walk with Him today and every day of your life.

Jesus has called upon believers of every generation (and that includes you) to follow in His footsteps. Will you follow? Please answer that question with a GREAT BIG YES. When you do, your heart will be filled with a GREAT BIG LOVE for Him!

A Thought for Today

Peter said, "No, Lord!" But he had to learn that one cannot say "No" while saying "Lord" and that one cannot say "Lord" while saying "No."

Corrie ten Boom

Pray for Everybody

Hatred stirs up trouble,
but love forgives all wrongs.

Proverbs 10:12 NCV

It's usually pretty easy to pray for your friends and family members—all you have to do is find the time. But when it comes to praying for people who have hurt you, well, that's a different matter entirely!

Like it or not, God says that you've got to pray for the folks you like and for the folks you don't like. Why? Well, maybe it's because God knows that He has already forgiven you, and now He thinks it's about time for you to forgive them.

A Thought for Today

Only the truly forgiven are truly forgiving.

C. S. Lewis

It's Good For You

So I recommend having fun, because there is nothing better for people to do in this world than to eat, drink, and enjoy life. That way they will experience some happiness along with all the hard work God gives them.

Ecclesiastes 8:15 NLT

Sometimes, we may feel guilty about having fun when some people around the world are not having any fun at all. But God doesn't want us to spend our lives moping around with frowns on our faces. Far from it! God tells us that a happy heart is a very good thing to have.

So if you're afraid to laugh out loud, don't be. Remember that God wouldn't have given you the gift of laughter if He hadn't intended for you to use it. And remember: if you're laughing, that does not mean that you're unconcerned about people who may be hurting. It simply means that you've taken a little time to have fun, and that's good because God wants you to have a cheerful heart.

When You Make a Mistake

If we claim that we're free of sin, we're only fooling ourselves. A claim like that is errant nonsense. On the other hand, if we admit our sins—make a clean breast of them—he won't let us down; he'll be true to himself. He'll forgive our sins and purge us of all wrongdoing.

1 John 1:8-9 MSG

Are you perfect? Of course not! Even if you're a very good person, you're bound to mistakes and lots of them.

When you make a mistake, you must try your best to learn from it (so that you won't make the very same mistake again). And, if you have hurt someone—or if you have disobeyed God—you must ask for forgiveness. And here's the good news: when you ask for God's forgiveness, He will always give it. God forgives you every single time you ask Him to. So ask!

God Knows Best

Trust God from the bottom of your heart;
don't try to figure out everything on your own.
Listen for God's voice in everything you do,
everywhere you go; he's the one
who will keep you on track.

Proverbs 3:5-6 MSG

Here are three things to think about: 1. God loves you. 2. God wants what's best for you. 3. God has a plan for you.

God's plan may not always happen exactly like you want, but remember: God always knows best. Sometimes, even though you may want something very badly, you must still be patient and wait for the right time to get it, And the right time, of course, is determined by God.

Even if you don't get exactly what you want today, you can be sure that God wants what's best for you . . . today, tomorrow, and forever.

Big Ideas About...

Helping Others

Here are two important ideas.
Take a few minutes to talk to your mom or dad
about what these quotations mean.

Encouraging others means
helping people, looking for
the best in them, and trying to
bring out their positive qualities.

John Maxwell

Make it a rule, and pray to God to help you to
keep it, never, if possible, to lie down at night
without being able to say: "I have made one
human being at least a little wiser, or a little
happier, or at least a little better this day."

Charles Kingsley

Always Growing

This is why I remind you to keep using
the gift God gave you when I laid
my hands on you. Now let it grow,
as a small flame grows into a fire.

2 Timothy 1:6 NCV

You're growing up day by day, and it's a wonderful thing to watch. Every day, you're learning new things and doing new things. Good for you!

And when should you stop growing up? Hopefully never! That way, you'll always be learning more and doing more.

Do you think it's good to keep growing and growing and growing? If you said "yes," you're right. So remember: you're a very special person today . . . and you'll be just as special when you've grown a little bit more tomorrow.

Today's Tip

Grown-ups still have plenty to learn . . . and so do you!

Happiness and Honesty

Lying lips are an abomination to the Lord,
but those who deal truthfully are His delight.
Proverbs 12:22 NKJV

Have you ever said something that wasn't true? When you did, were you sorry for what you had said? Probably so.

When we're dishonest, we make ourselves unhappy in surprising ways. Here are just a few troubles that result from dishonesty: we feel guilty, we are usually found out, we disappoint others, and we disappoint God. It's easy to see that lies always cause more problems than they solve.

Happiness and honesty always go hand in hand. But it's up to you to make sure that you go hand in hand with them!

Today's Tip

When telling the truth is hard . . . it probably means that you're afraid of what others might think—or what they might do—if you're truthful. But even when telling the truth is hard, it's always the right thing to do.

God's Angels

Don't neglect to show hospitality,
for by doing this some have welcomed angels
as guests without knowing it.

Hebrews 13:2 HCSB

The Bible has a lot to say about angels. But
maybe you've wondered if angels are really real.
If so, wonder no more! If the Bible tells you
something, you can be sure that it's true.

The Bible teaches us that angels come from
God, so that means they are good and they are
helpful. So, we don't need to fear angels . . .
but neither do we need to pretend that they
don't exist!

A Thought for Today

I believe in angels because the Bible says
there are angels; and I believe the Bible
to be the true Word of God.

Billy Graham

The Time to Talk to God Is Now

Always be happy. Never stop praying.
Give thanks whatever happens. That is what
God wants for you in Christ Jesus.

1 Thessalonians: 5:16-18 ICB

God promises that He hears your prayers—
every one of them! So, if you want to say
something to God, you can start praying (with
your eyes open or shut).

Whatever your need, no matter how great
or small, pray about it and never lose hope. God
is not just near; He is here, and He's ready to
talk with you. Now!

Today's Tip

Sometimes, the answer to prayer is "No." God
doesn't grant all of our requests, nor should
He.

Don't Be Afraid to Ask Questions

When doubts filled my mind, your comfort
gave me renewed hope and cheer.

Psalm 94:19 NLT

When you're not sure about something, are
you willing to ask your parents what you should
do? Hopefully, when you have a question,
you're not afraid to ask.

If you've got lots of questions, the Bible
promises that God—like your parents—has
answers, too.

So don't ever be afraid to ask questions.
Both your parents and your Heavenly Father
want to hear your questions . . . and they want
to answer your questions as soon as you ask.

Today's Tip

When in doubt, ask mom or dad. If you're not
sure whether or not something is right or
wrong, ask a parent before you do it!

Self-Control Matters

So prepare your minds for service and have
self-control. All your hope should be for
the gift of grace that will be yours when
Jesus Christ is shown to you.

1 Peter 1:13 NCV

Learning how to control yourself is an
important part of growing up. The more you
learn about self-control, the better. Self-
control will help you at home, at school, and at
church. That's why parents and teachers are
happy to talk about the rewards of good self-
control. And that's why you should be excited
about learning how important it is to look
before you leap . . . not after!

Today's Tip

Sometimes, the best way to control yourself
is to slow yourself down. Then, you can think
about the things you're about to do before you
do them.

Waiting Until the Time is Right

He has made everything beautiful in its time.
Ecclesiastes 3:11 NIV

Sometimes, the hardest thing to do is to wait. This is especially true when we're in a hurry and when we want things to happen now, if not sooner! But God's plan does not always happen in the way that we would like or at the time of our own choosing. Still, God always knows best.

Sometimes, even though we may want something very badly, we must still be patient and wait for the right time to get it, And the right time, of course, is determined by God, not by us.

Today's Tip

Even when you want events to unfold according to your own timetable, it is important to trust God's timetable.

Big Ideas About...

The Words You Speak

Here are two important ideas.
Take a few minutes to talk to your mom or dad
about what these quotations mean.

I still believe we ought to talk about Jesus.
The old country doctor of my boyhood days
always began his examination by saying,
"Let me see your tongue." That's a good way
to check a Christian: the tongue test.
Let's hear what he is talking about.

Vance Havner

Change the heart,
and you change the speech.

Warren Wiersbe

When To Do Your Homework

We can't afford to waste a minute, must not
squander these precious daylight hours in
frivolity and indulgence, in sleeping around and
dissipation, in bickering and grabbing everything
in sight. Get out of bed and get dressed!
Don't loiter and linger, waiting until the very
last minute. Dress yourselves in Christ,
and be up and about!

Romans 13:13-14 MSG

Sooner or later, you'll start getting
homework, and when that day comes, you'd
better be ready because that's when you'll really
need lots of self-control! Usually, homework
isn't hard to do, but it takes time. And
sometimes, we'd rather be doing other things
(like playing outside or watching TV). But, when
we put off our homework until the last possible
minute, we make it hard on ourselves.

Instead of putting off your homework, do it
first. Then, you'll have the rest of your time to
have fun—and you won't have to worry about
all that homework.

Telling The Truth

Don't ever forget kindness and truth.
Wear them like a necklace.
Write them on your heart as if on a tablet.
Proverbs 3:3 NCV

When we're dishonest, we make ourselves unhappy and we let other people down. It's easy to see that lies always cause far more problems than they solve. Lies, no matter what size, are never part of God's plan for our lives, so we must tell the truth about everything.

Have you ever said something that wasn't true? When you did, were you sorry for what you had said? Probably so.

Happiness and honesty always go hand in hand. But it's up to you to make sure that you go hand in hand with them! And besides, when you always tell the truth, you don't have to try and remember what it was that you said!

An Attitude of Kindness

Finally, all of you should be of one mind,
full of sympathy toward each other,
loving one another with tender hearts
and humble minds.

1 Peter 3:8 NLT

An attitude of kindness starts in your heart and works it's way out from there.

Do you listen to your heart when it tells you to be kind to other people? Hopefully, you do. After all, lots of people in the world aren't as fortunate as you are—and some of these folks are living very near you.

Ask your parents to help you find ways to do nice things for other people. And don't forget that everybody needs love, kindness, and respect, so you should always be ready to share those things, too.

Listening to Directions

A fool's way is right in his own eyes,
but whoever listens to counsel is wise.
Proverbs 12:15 HCSB

Directions, directions, directions. It seems like somebody is always giving you directions: telling you where to go, how to behave, and what to do next. But sometimes all these directions can be confusing! How can you understand everything that everybody tells you? The answer, of course, is that you must pay careful attention to those directions . . . and that means listening.

To become a careful listener, here are some things you must do: 1. Don't talk when you're supposed to be listening (your ears work best when your mouth is closed); 2. Watch the person who's giving the directions (when your eyes and ears work together, it's easier to understand things); 3. If you don't understand something, ask a question (it's better to ask now than to make a mistake later).

Today, Try to Memorize This Verse

Surely goodness and mercy
shall follow me
all the days of my life:
and I will dwell
in the house of the Lord for ever.

Psalm 23:6 KJV

Here's a Bible verse that you should learn.
Practice saying it several times.
And then, talk to mom or dad
about exactly what the verse means.

Learning to Be More Obedient

Here is my final advice:
Honor God and obey his commands.

Ecclesiastes 12:13 ICB

Learning how to control yourself helps you become a more obedient person. So the more you learn about self-control, the better.

Learning how to control yourself is a good thing. Self-control helps you at home, at school, and at church. That's why parents and teachers are happy to talk about the rewards of good behavior.

If you want to learn more about self-control, ask your parents. They'll help you figure out better ways to behave yourself. And that's good for everybody . . . especially you!

Today's Tip

Be patient, and follow the rules . . . even if you don't like some of the rules that you're supposed to follow, follow them anyway.

What Is Patience?

We urge you, brethren, admonish the unruly,
encourage the fainthearted,
help the weak, be patient with everyone.
1 Thessalonians 5:14 NASB

The dictionary defines the word patience
as "the ability to be calm, tolerant, and
understanding." Here's what that means: the
word "calm" means being in control of your
emotions (not letting your emotions control
you). The word "tolerant" means being kind and
considerate to people who are different from
you. And, the word "understanding" means
being able to put yourself in another person's
shoes.

If you can be calm, tolerant, and
understanding, you will be the kind of person
whose good deeds are a blessing to your family
and friends. And that's exactly the kind of
person that God wants you to be.

Kindness is a Choice

Love is patient; love is kind.

1 Corinthians 13:4 HCSB

Kindness is a choice. Sometimes, when we feel happy or hopeful, we find it easy to be kind. Other times, when we are sad or tired, we may find it much harder to be kind. But the Bible teaches us to be kind, even when we don't feel like it.

So do everybody (including yourself) a big favor: try to be kind all the time. It's the smart choice and the right thing to do.

Today's Tip

Kindness should be part of our lives every day, not just on the days when we feel good. And remember: small acts of kindness can make a big difference.

Do the Right Thing . . .
And the Kind Thing

Let everyone see that you are gentle and kind.
The Lord is coming soon.

Philippians 4:5 NCV

Sometimes, it's so much easier to do the wrong thing than it is to do the right thing, especially when we're tired or frustrated. But, doing the wrong thing almost always leads to trouble. And sometimes, it leads to BIG trouble.

When you do the right thing, you don't have to worry about what you did or what you said. But, when you do the wrong thing, you'll be worried that someone will find out. So do the right thing, which, by the way, also happens to be the kind thing. You'll be glad you did, and so will other people!

A Thought for Today

When you launch an act of kindness out into the crosswinds of life, it will blow kindness back to you.

Dennis Swanberg

How To Treat Others

So let us try to do what makes peace
and helps one another.

Romans 14:19 NCV

Would you like to make the world a better
place? If so, you can start by practicing the
Golden Rule.

Jesus said, "Whatever you want others
to do for you, do also the same for them"
(Matthew 7:12 HCSB). That means that you
should treat other people in the very same way
that you want to be treated. That's the Golden
Rule.

So here's what you should do: if you want
to know how to treat somebody, ask the person
you see when you look into the mirror. The
answer you get will tell you exactly what to do.

Today's Tip

When you're trying to decide how to treat
another person, ask yourself this question:
"How would I feel if somebody treated me that
way?" Then, treat the other person the way
that you would want to be treated.

Learning the Importance of Obedience

Therefore whoever hears these sayings of
Mine, and does them, I will liken him to
a wise man who built his house on the rock:
and the rain descended, the floods came,
and the winds blew and beat on that house;
and it did not fall, for it was founded
on the rock.

Matthew 7:24-25 NKJV

When you learn to control your actions
and your words, you will find it easier to obey
your parents, your teachers, and your Father
in heaven. Why? Because in order to be an
obedient person, you must first learn how to
control yourself—otherwise, you won't be able
to obey very well, even when you want to.

When you learn the importance of
obedience, you'll soon discover that good
things happen when you behave yourself. And
the sooner you learn to listen and obey, the
sooner those good things will start happening.

Want More Patience? God Can Help!

God has chosen you and made you his holy people. He loves you. So always do these things: Show mercy to others, be kind, humble, gentle, and patient.

Colossians 3:12 NCV

Are you a perfectly patient person? If so, feel free to skip the rest of this page. But if you're not, here's something to think about: If you really want to become a more patient person, God is ready and willing to help.

God is always ready to help you become a better person. In fact, the Bible promises that when you sincerely seek God's help, He will give you the things you need. So, if you want to become a more patient person, bow your head and start praying about it. Then, rest assured that with God's help, you can change for the better . . . and you will!

Big Ideas About...

Celebrating Today

Here are two important ideas.
Take a few minutes to talk to your mom or dad
about what these quotations mean.

Don't waste today's time
cluttering up tomorrow's
opportunities with
yesterday's troubles.

Barbara Johnson

With each new dawn, life delivers
a package to your front door,
rings your doorbell, and runs.

Charles Swindoll

Changing Habits

Do not be deceived:
"Evil company corrupts good habits."
1 Corinthians 15:33 NKJV

Most people have a few habits they'd like to change, and maybe you do, too. If so, God can help.

If you trust God, and if you keep asking Him to help you change bad habits, He will help you make yourself into a new person. So, if at first you don't succeed, keep praying. God is listening, and He's ready to help you become a better person if you ask Him . . . so ask Him!

Today's Tip

The old saying is familiar and true: "First you make your habits; then your habits make you." So it's always a good time to ask this question: "What kind of person are my habits making me?"

God's Greatest Promise

I assure you:
Anyone who believes has eternal life.

John 6:47 HCSB

It's time to remind yourself of a promise that God made a long time ago—the promise that God sent His Son Jesus to save the world and to save you! And when you stop to think about it, there can be no greater promise than that.

No matter where you are, God is with you. God loves you, and He sent His Son so that you can live forever in heaven with your loved ones. WOW! That's the greatest promise in the history of the universe. The End.

A Thought for Today

The unfolding of our friendship with the Father will be a never-ending revelation stretching on into eternity.

Catherine Marshall